Crystalline Moments

Discover Your Opportunities and Create Your Best Self

Coni K. Meyers

ISBN 13: 978-0-9968997-2-7
ISBN 10: 0-9968997-2-3

Printed in the United States of America

www.CrystallineMoments.com

Book cover design by Sandy Warburton and Marti Green

I dedicate this book to my husband, Tom, to all seven of our children, their spouses and to my amazing grandchildren.

To the rest of my family and the incredible friends that I have, just know that without all of your love and support, this book and my new path as a Life Mastery Consultant, would not have been possible.

A very special thank you to everyone that was willing to share their stories so that others might learn how to find opportunity in their own Crystalline Moments.

And finally, to Mary Morrissey for being a guiding spiritual light in my life for over 25 years.

"Have Fun, Give Back, Make Money"

~Coni K. Meyers

To clarify the terms, *higher power, Universe, intuition, God, little voice, mindset, 'Aha' moments* or *guardian angel*s discussed throughout this book as *Crystalline Moments*, please feel free to substitute your own personal spiritual belief system into the definition of each story told.

Crystalline Moments happen universally to everyone, young or old, male or female, regardless of your interpretation.

Table of Contents

Foreword

"Have you ever had a flash of blinding clarity that completely transformed your life forever? These alchemical events are what Coni Meyers calls "crystalline moments."

Crystalline moments are not just moments of clarity - they are events that are so extraordinarily compelling that you choose to take your life in an entirely new direction. It's as if you have emerged from a closed chrysalis state—the emerging butterfly can never be a caterpillar again.

Crystalline moments often meld pain and suffering with joy and happiness. For example, there can be beauty and joy coupled with death. It doesn't mean that you don't experience the pain of the loss; instead, you experience an enlightening where the transformative process begins and the pain begins to fade away.

Crystalline Moments is a collection of life-altering stories that span the range of human experience from childhood to death. Like life's crystalline moments, these stories will bring you joy, make you cry, and may even make you angry. Most importantly, however, as you encounter these alchemical events on your personal journey, *Crystalline Moments* is your handbook for living a happier and more fulfilling life."

Bernice Ross, PH.D.
Nationally syndicated columnist, author, speaker and consultant

Testimonials

"Crystalline Moments are gifts sometimes disguised as challenges, sometimes just thoughts, but those moments are a time to expand and grow. Coni's book shows how to find the opportunity in those moments we all have."
Mary Morrissey, life coach, motivational speaker,
spiritual author and Founder of Life Mastery Institute

"Coni has written an inspiring and motivational book that will encourage you to identify and take advantage of your own Crystalline Moments. Here you'll find first-hand accounts of how people turned challenges and opportunities into triumphs and the lessons we can apply to our own lives."
Edward Segal, author of Getting Your 15 Minutes of Fame and More! *and* Profit by Publicity: The How-to Reference Guide for Real Estate Agents & Brokers

"Coni Meyers has been an expert and authority in the personal success industry for many years. Her book, "Crystalline Moments", reveals the truth about all of us. We each have key moments in life of accomplishment, love, and contentment...it's how we approach, apply, and take action after having those moments that manifest a better life. Coni has captured thought and action and blended powerful stories of other elite and successful people to illustrate a road map to success."
Dirk Zeller, best-selling author of 10 books
CEO, Real Estate Champions, Inc.

"As I've ventured through my life, it has always amazed me how talented, successful people have ventured through theirs. I've known Coni for so many years and yet never realized the life-changing event that was going to move her to pen this book. I found myself with a new respect for a friend and fellow colleague...Write on, Coni and Read on folks! Gratitude is a beautiful thing."
Gail Hartnett, REALTOR®, Boise, Idaho
2006 National President Women's Council of Realtors

"I highly recommend Crystalline Moments.
While reading this book, I recognized my own "AHA" moments that put me on the track to where I am today-a path I would have never imagined. The stories display how important it is to be open to life's experiences and allow them to point us in the right direction.

Like everyone, I have experienced my own pain and loss- many difficult times I thought I would never get through. Yet looking back, I realized that these experiences always led to new passions once I learned to accept what the Universe was presenting."
Deborah Falcone
Real Estate | Vertical Markets
Real Estate Director, The Wall Street Journal

"Coni's book captures and connects us all to the fragility of life experiences with people from all walks of life. Their stories share how a single moment in time changed the trajectory of their lives and how they were able to harness the power of their thinking, tragic or triumphant, to grow and prosper. This book will help you connect to your own moments of power to discover your Crystalline Moments through authentic examples of power, grace and peace."
Terri Murphy, speaker, best-selling author, trainer
Producer of ISucceed.com
Executive Director of Women's Wisdom Network

"There are times in your life when you reach a crossroad. You can choose the path that honors your spirit and passion. Even through the most difficult of times, when you have lost all faith and hope, you have a choice. Crystalline Moments are those times of clarity and purpose when you finally realize or wake up to your true passion in life. When you choose to pursue that path, believe and trust in yourself, ALL THINGS ARE POSSIBLE.

Coni's Crystalline Moment came at the passing of her beloved husband. I have watched her emerge a stronger, beautiful, radiant person. She has the ability to "see" the potential in others and help them define their Crystalline Moments. I am so excited that she has written this book and is able to share her skills with others. I believe she will be a guide for many people to discover their very own Crystalline Moments."
Dawn Lane, CEO/President
Hope Home Foundation

"It has been a privilege to cheer Coni on as she explores and defines her new life and helps others do the same. She is a truly old soul with the ability to both guide and lead others in their own quest for their best path.

When I met Coni, she was dealing with some of life's toughest challenges with grace and dignity.

Coni always took the time to be a good friend, even while she coped with the many hard blows that led to the loss of her amazing husband. Even at that time, in her darkest hours, I saw life beckoning with a new road for Coni.

The stories in the book both resonate and give true inspiration. If you are in need of inspiration, comfort or insight, you have come to the right place."
Janet Choynowski
CEO, Immobel Group

"Coni has done a wonderful job identifying and describing Crystalline Moments in her collection of personal stories. We have all experienced these moments or turning points in our lives at one time or another, and the collective sharing of these stories reinforces the knowingness we all desire to see, feel and know - a power greater than ourselves!"
Sherri Souza, REALTOR® Broker In Trust
WCR National Recording Secretary, 2015
CA WCR State President, 2011

Introduction

Have you had a Crystalline Moment? Of course you have...you just may not have known it. Oprah and many others describe these as "Aha" moments. How I came about using the term crystalline moment was a Crystalline Moment in itself. A dear friend of mine used it to describe an unforgettable occurrence in her life and the minute I heard it, it resonated deep within me. A new truth had been uncovered. You know when you connect with something within that is undeniable, no matter what anyone says or does, there is no disputing this truth, and that is what happened to me.

I like to call them crystalline because they are moments of clarity. Webster Dictionary defines crystalline as: "strikingly clear or sparkling". In these moments of clarity is where we find life opportunities.

In the process of researching for my book, I looked up "crystalline moments" and found a great story from a motorcycle magazine writer named Jeff Buchanan. He shares, "I was suddenly overcome by a feeling of absolute contentment. I thought to myself, how could this moment be any better? I was on the perfect bike. I was with the woman I wanted to be with, and we were in a beautiful part of the world. I felt this couldn't get any better even if I was the richest man in the world." In the article, he calls this his Crystalline Moment.

I then came across Aron Ralston's story. He was the climber that had to make the decision to cut his arm off in order to free himself from being stuck in a crevice, and subsequently, the movie, *127 Hours*, was made about his ordeal. He calls that moment a Crystalline Moment. This made it resonate with me at a deeper level. Crystalline Moments had a definite hold on me.

Sometimes it is truly a moment; other times it's a period of time but the common thread is that they are moments that are memorable and they will always be a part of our existence. It is what we do during these times that is the important part. If we just ignore them, they can cause us distress later, or we may not enjoy the moment as much as we should.

You will hear Mary Morrissey's story later but she writes that, "In that moment, no matter good or bad, there is a perfect moment for expansion and deepening of ourselves." Crystalline Moments are typically unexpected and pivotal so you must be open to the possibility when that little "voice" speaks to you.

We all have our own stories. Some of us find opportunities and take full advantage of them, and some of us dismiss them and keep on walking down our usual path. Our life will always move forward but we are no longer in the driver's seat. We all have 525,600 minutes in a year. What are you going to do with that time? We can either write the story of our life and design it, or let our conditions and circumstances dictate and create a constant default. I dared myself to listen to my inner voice. I dared myself to start designing. I found the courage to move forward to design the life I wanted to live.

My book chronicles stories from people who have had all kinds of moments, including mine. You are going to experience, no matter how painful it may be, that opportunities in Crystalline Moments abound.

****

I was very ill as a child and had been in and out of hospitals with kidney problems. For my 10th birthday, my mother took me to work with her. She worked for Baldwin Manufacturing in Kearney, Nebraska. I spent the morning opening birthday presents from everyone in the company. Seeing three long tables filled with gifts was a dream! But the best birthday present was when the owners of the company - huge contributors to the Mayo Clinic who even have the Baldwin Building named after them - handed my parents a check to take me to the Mayo Clinic. It saved my life.

I had been told that I was going to be fine after a procedure they administered to me. I only had to stay in the hospital one night and I was in a room with a girl a couple years older than me. We shared the same kidney disease, however, hers was much more advanced. She had no control of her body, speech, bodily functions...nothing. In watching her, I realized that I was being given a gift. I'm not sure how this thought came to me. I do remember thinking I needed to be very good and take care of others since I was taken care of and was going to get well.

I can still remember the room, the girl, the bed, the smell...it was that intense. This moment defined my deep-rooted desire to help those in need. Ask anyone that knows me; I used to do it to a fault. It wasn't until recently that I connected the dots that my desire to give came from a place of fear rather than from a loving place of wonder and love. This realization was a Crystalline Moment.

After this Crystalline Moment, I decided to learn more about my journey. I sat down and gave myself space to be and think of the defining moments in that stage of my life. Here is what came to me.

After getting out of the Mayo Clinic, I wanted to go back to school. Like in Little House on the Prairie, I went to a one-room school house that consisted of 10 kids. Because I had been so sick and always had problems making it to the bathroom on time, I would have accidents all the time. You would think I would feel ridiculed by the other nine students, but it was the embarrassment the adults felt that, needless to say, put shame in me. I grew timid, shy and petrified of groups of people.

That first week, I had to get up in front of the WHOLE school, all nine of them, and give a story report. I can tell you that there were hot dogs and potatoes sitting on top of the oil stove, that it was sunshiny outside, that I was wearing a polka dot dress and what the room smelled like at the time. I was terrified! I couldn't talk. I stuttered and did not do well with the report.

Our teacher's name was Mrs. Headlee, who we called Headless Headlee because she was very mean to everyone. As soon as I sat down, she got up in front of everyone and said, "Do you know who has the highest IQ in this school and who just gave the worst story report?"

From that moment on, I always felt that no matter how well I did something, it was never going to be good enough and that I didn't deserve any praise. I was crystal clear on that point. I bought into that belief.

I became an adult and had huge success in the real estate and insurance industries. My family would celebrate and be so proud of me. In a very painful space inside, I did not get it at all. Why could I not be happy? All I could think was, I do not deserve this. Why? Because I was hard wired that no matter how hard I worked, I did not deserve any recognition for my accomplishments. My crystalline moment occurred as I connected the dots from how I felt in that little school to how similar it felt to have all this success. I was a grown woman stuck in my old ways of thinking. I was an adult living a life from how I felt when I was 10.

In reading this book, you are going to hear everything from how people have overcome the loss of loved ones, to someone winning a $34 million lottery and everything betwixt and between.

You will learn how to identify the opportunities that these Crystalline Moments offer and how to take advantage of them. You will also learn how to overcome moments that you have not dealt with from your past.

Wishing you love and gentleness as you uncover your own potential to see your Crystalline Moments.

My Story

Why did I decide to write this book?

I had an amazing life, a great husband and we shared seven incredible children. He had three girls and one boy from his previous marriage and I had three boys. We shared two homes - my dream home in Portland and his dream home in Las Vegas. We would travel together and it was a great time in our marriage of 24 years. He was working with his kids in Vegas and loved it. I was a principal in a company I loved in Portland. Everything was great! It all seemed so balanced. It was an untraditional dynamic relationship, but one that created love, joy, communion and great communication not only between the two of us, but between us and our children.

I was at a convention at New Orleans in October 2010 when that great life would suddenly be washed away with the news that my husband had cancer. I put my job on hold and within a few days, I was at my husband's side. My focus became entirely on Tom getting well. As a family, we were doing everything possible to find the best care for him. His daughter, Sherrie, was his medical advocate and I took care of his personal needs while the rest of the family provided love and support.

We didn't know for months what kind of cancer he had. We just knew he was not getting well. It was doctor's visits, tests and more tests...an emotional roller coaster as the doctors tried to determine what kind of cancer he had.

One of the things I learned during this period of time is that you have friends you would never know existed. People that we only slightly knew stepped into our lives to offer unconditional presence.

Finally in January 2011, the doctors determined it was a rare form of liver cancer and that there was no known cure. Tom's spirit was not daunted. He wanted to go to San Diego for his birthday in February. I was thrilled and loved his tenacity to even want to share the driving responsibilities a portion of the way there.

All of his kids, his sister and brother-in-law and niece and her fiancé joined us in a beautiful home on the water in Oceanside. Tom loved deep sea fishing, and as a matter of fact, on our first date we went out fishing off the coast of Camarillo, CA. It was one of the things we loved to do together. We went to his favorite place where the boats dock and to his favorite little restaurant for fish. I watched him as he walked around with his family all surrounding him.

It was only when he started reading all the funny birthday cards that he started to cry. "You are trying to make this old man cry," he said, full of emotion. It was the first time in all those years that I had ever seen him shed a tear. I cannot even convey the emotions that I had during that moment. I was sad and terrified of what was to come and at the same time, I was filled with love for this man that I had known for 25 years. I knew by next year on this date of February 11, he would not be on this earth. It was one of the saddest moments in my life.

During the journey back to Vegas, we talked about our anniversary. We were going to celebrate our 25th anniversary but it was not until September. Even though I wanted to believe that everything was going to be ok, every bone in my body knew he would not make it that long. So I asked him how he felt about celebrating in March. I told him how important it would be to me and how great it would be to have all seven kids together for it. The real reason was because I wanted the family to be together one last time. We had not had all the kids together ever since the day we got married. There was always one missing from family occasions. He agreed that it would be nice, although I know he only did it for me. I talked to everyone and they changed whatever plans they had to make sure they were here. We set the date for March 19th.

As Tom grew weaker, it became more difficult for him to be up and get around. We tried to talk Tom into having a hospital bed downstairs, but he insisted on staying in our master bedroom, so the kids installed a chairlift so he could go up and down the stairs with ease. They also got him a wheelchair and walker. While we were making plans for the party, he was having a lot of difficulty getting up and down from the bed until it reached the point where he could not use the walker anymore.

A friend of mine who had worked as a counselor for an AIDS clinic offered me the best advice anyone could have who is going through this with someone they love. "Every day, find something to laugh about," she told me. Tom and I did, sometimes at his expense, but we laughed about something every day. This one night in particular we laughed until we cried.

After he started losing the use of his legs, I would tell him not to get up by himself at night, to wake me up so I could help. I'd even moved his walker away from the bed so he couldn't reach it. He didn't want to wake me this one night, so he decided to get up and go to the bathroom. He'd somehow managed to sit himself up on the edge of the bed. "Coni, I need your help!" he cried out. I woke up and ran to the other side of the bed just as he slid onto the floor. Unlike many cancer patients that lose a lot of weight, Tom had not. He still weighed over 200 pounds and now was sitting on the floor. My 5'2" body finally got him on all fours and slowly over to the loveseat so I could push his butt up onto it. "I'm sure glad there are no cameras in this room!" he said, as I tried to raise him up. We both burst out laughing and just sat there on the floor holding our sides.

It was during this time that I would experience a devastating Crystalline Moment. Even though you have been told that someone you love is going to die, you still hold out hope against hope. It was finally time to call hospice and they came out for the initial interview.

Earlier that day, an attorney had come to the house to make sure that all of his affairs were in order. I made it through the appointment with the attorney, but it was only about two hours later the hospice people showed up. That was it! That was the moment! It hit me that I was not going to have this man in my life and I couldn't take it. I had to leave the room. It was as painful as any pain I had ever felt and I wanted to run away. Unfortunately, it is not the kind of pain you can run from or take a pill and feel better. It is a pain that puts you into another dimension and you just have to let the pain happen. But you have a job to do and you put your attention on what matters. For me, it was my husband's comfort. But the clarity of the moment did not leave my being. Besides, we still had a party to plan.

The day of the party came. All the kids but one had arrived. Earlier, I had teased him, asking if he would wear his silk pajamas so he could be like Hugh Hefner. He chuckled and got a twinkle in his eye. I had been saving six bottles of 1996 Dom Pérignon champagne that I acquired several years earlier for a very special occasion. It's amazing how the Universe plans for us! I knew there was never going to be a more special day than this.

Tom did great and was able to stay up for several hours. The next day, my son who couldn't make it earlier, came to say goodbye. As soon as he left, Tom started going downhill. He'd hung on to say goodbye to all of our children.

A few days later, Tom was gone. My life as I had known it had drastically changed...I had changed. The man I had loved, laughed and fought with was gone. After Tom passed, I spent time wrapped in all the memories of the life we had led. It had not always been perfect...there were plenty of ups and downs, but the last six months were the best time we had together. For many nights after, I wore one of his shirts to bed just to be able to smell him and feel that he was around me. It was very comforting to have his scent while I slept. I still have his silk pajamas and one of his favorite Columbia fish shirts hanging in the closet. It feels good to know there is still a physical part of him in the closet.

I did do one thing that would later become the engine that would turn my life around. I realized that by becoming unconditional to him in his time of need, all beauty fell into place. What if I would learn to live my life from that loving space? Even though I was in blinding pain, I fell into deep gratitude for the choice I made to dedicate all of my time to him during his illness.

Little did I know how much my life was about to still change.

They say that the biggest blows in life are suffering the loss of a loved one, losing your job or losing your home. Would you believe me if I told you, shortly after Tom's death, that I experienced all three?

When the doctors had called to tell us that Tom had cancer that October, I had told everyone at my work that I was going to be concentrating on Tom until he was well. I wanted to give Tom all of my attention and be of complete service to him.

Because I traveled to Oregon, California and Nevada for work, I was on the road a lot. As a matter of fact, when I first got to Vegas that October, Tom kept asking me about what my plans were. It took him two or three months before he realized I wasn't going anywhere. I kept telling him I would be with him until he was well but he didn't believe me. You see, my normal life philosophy was work, work, work. If I didn't have something else to do, I was working. He used to beg me not to work so many hours.

Now that he was gone, the first thing I thought of doing was getting back to work. I tried to pick up the pieces and I thought, "Ok, I will just start calling people and will be back into it in no time and that would be the best thing for me."

Wrong! It didn't take me long to realize that everything was different. I tried talking to my partners and when they would talk about work, I wasn't even hearing what they were saying. When I would try and talk to people about our business - online education - it was like I was listening from the outside and wasn't a part of the conversation.

Now the realization hits me that the life I had known was gone - that I was not the same person that had been at that convention in New Orleans just a few short months ago.

Thanks to family and friends, I wasn't alone but I was definitely lost. I had never felt this way before. What do I do now? Do I stay in Vegas or go back to Portland? Where was my home going to be?

For the next nine months, one minute I would be staying in Vegas and the next I would be going back to Portland. This was taking an incredible toll on me. The Thursday after Christmas, I woke up and the first thought I had was that I was going to stay in Vegas. It was an absolute moment of clarity and the decision was made. Doubt no longer clouded my mind.

I knew that meant that I was giving up my dream home in Portland. This was the home that, with the help of my mother's inheritance, I had transformed into everything I had ever wanted.

That same morning, I called my partners in Oregon to tell them of my decision. I could tell they were not happy about it, but I also had to do what was right for me. Sometimes when these moments happen, there is going to be chaos before there is clarity of what that means for your life. I felt sad but happy at the same time. I had no clue where this journey was going to take me, but I knew this was the first step.

The following Tuesday, my partners called me to tell me that they wanted to dissolve the relationship. I'd just lost my husband, was giving up my dream home, and now I was without a job. Soon I would be out of the company that I had helped build and loved. This also meant that there was no money to continue the mortgage payments on the home in Portland. Ultimately, I would lose my dream home.

As I set about selling all my 'stuff' in Portland, I realized that my actions represented shedding everything so I could start a brand new life. I didn't see what was next yet, but what I knew for sure, this was an incredible opportunity. During that nine

13

months after I lost my husband, the death of my old life happened and I was birthing a new life. WOW!! What a Crystalline Moment!

'How' I was going to get to this new life was still unknown but 'Why' I was going in this direction made total sense to me.

There was no turning back. The Crystalline Moments were too numerous to count during that period of time. But it is just like when you learn to play a new sport or game. The more you pay attention, the easier it is to recognize the next step. Step by step, I was breathing into my new life.

Sherrie and I talked about what I was going to do. I told her I needed a new philosophy about life, that my previous philosophy of work, work, work no longer fit. Then it hit me. I wanted to have fun, give back and make money. Aha! Another moment of clarity!

A great follower of Mary Morrissey, a spiritual leader and philosopher for many years, I received her inspirational messages every morning.

I started getting emails about her coaching program. I ignored them at first, then one morning I saw another email about her DreamBuilder coaching program. This time the message had a different energy around it. I had allowed myself to dream about all of the things I would love to do and had made a list. This message popped out of the computer and into my face - almost like it slapped me. Maybe I could be a coach!

As soon as I let that thought cross my mind, my next thoughts were, "Oh, wait a minute. You don't know anything about coaching. What makes you think you could do that?" The pull of the message became stronger than my ability to delete it. I picked up the phone and called.

While talking to their representative about the program, something happened. I started to feel really comfortable. My heart became lighter than it had been in years. Could I really become a life coach, did I have what it took, and what made me think that I did?

Those thoughts were followed by the truth about myself. I'd always loved being a sales manager. I trained and coached hundreds of people in sales and marketing. I enjoyed the feeling of helping someone else succeed.

I filled out a questionnaire to see if I qualified for their program. Once I completed that and during my next conversation with them, a moment of clarity happened again.

YES! I could be a life coach! Now I had to commit to the money. SCARY!! One of the things that I didn't know at the time is that if your energy is in alignment with your dream, it is not important at the moment to know how it is going to happen; it will become apparent.

The money suddenly showed up!

In October 2010, if someone would have said that I would be writing a book and become a prestigious Life Mastery Consultant serving others, I would have said you were crazy. "Have fun, give back, make money" is a wonderful philosophy that is serving me much better than work, work, work!

My Crystalline Moments created the opportunities that have manifested this amazing new life that I am leading. When you experience a moment of clarity, the secret is to stop what you are doing, listen to that inner voice and take the one little baby step that is in front of you.

In the years since Tom passed, I know that he has been my guide and many of the things he wanted for me have happened. I still feel him in our bedroom. There are many things I miss, and one of them is hearing his voice. Tom would always come up with Roses are red, Violets are blue poems for me. The last Mother's Day before he passed, he recorded a poem and sent it to me via a text message. I am so grateful for this as I can still hear his voice when I want to.

His kids also gave me an incredible gift the Mother's Day after he passed.

A few years before Tom became ill, I had flipped the pickup truck on its top driving from Vegas to Los Angeles. After the accident, whenever I was on the road and I would talk to Tom, he would always end the conversation by saying, "Keep the sunny side up. I love you, Babe."

A few weeks after Tom passed, I was invited to be a guest at a retreat/conference where I knew I would run into many familiar faces. The morning I was leaving to drive to Scottsdale for the event, I got in my car and realized that I was never going to hear those words again. Sherrie called me to see how I was doing driving. I was in tears and told her the story. She ended the conversation with, "We love you, keep the sunny side up." Even writing this today I still come to tears.

Mother's Day was just a couple weeks later and the kids went together and gave me a charm to hang in my car. It has a small heart frame with a picture of Tom on one side and me and Tom on the other. It also has another charm that says:

Keep the sunny side up. I love you babe...

1 GINNY DEHENNY

"Yes, you can go on!"

My first intimate conversation is with an absolutely amazing woman who has overcome grief beyond anything imaginable. Her story is of strength, courage and proof that out of the depths of despair, amazing things can happen.

****

Ginny Dehenny lost her son, Kelty, at age 17 to suicide and then their daughter, Riley, just years later.

Kelty was a happy energetic young man. He was an athlete and a good student. In a very short period of time, he declined into a deep depression. He struggled while his family did everything they could to help him. He hung himself after leaving a note to his family.

Eight years later, Riley was in Thailand studying yoga and massage. She had dislocated her shoulder and had been given pain medication that, as it turned out, was too strong for her. She died of a heart attack. Riley was only 23 years old.

I met Ginny at a conference where we sat on a panel together. Her story affected me deeply. Especially because it had only been a short time, a few weeks actually, since I had lost my husband. Her strength and insight is apparent in what she has done with her grief.

Coni: After my husband passed, I started talking to other people who have suffered loss, then I heard your story. Yours is a story of moving forward and such bravery. When people lose loved ones, some people find a way to move forward but many others just get stuck.

Ginny: Yes, you can go on. The one thing in life is that you have a choice of Option A or Option B. I'm a strong believer that everything happens for a reason and your strength comes from within. For me, there was no other option but to move forward.

Coni: When did you decide to start the foundation? Was this after Riley's death?

Ginny: No, this was after Kelty's death. We were in the hospital. Kelty was on life support. They had told us that he wasn't going to make it and we would have to take him off of life support. You're in this surreal environment because you can't believe what's happening.

I told the ICU doctor, Kelty would want to give back as an organ donor, which ended up saving eight other people's lives. We had already decided to start this foundation. In his obituary, we put in to donate to the foundation even though we hadn't really set it up yet. Kelty died March 2, 2001. We had our first board meeting shortly after with family.

We talked about how if we could raise $25,000, we could help a lot of people. Well, we've raised $7 million and helped hundreds and hundreds of people. When I went and talked to my doctor, Kelty was there with me. I didn't have the strength to move forward.

Kelty is what kept me going...my little guardian angel on my shoulder. Never in my life did I think I'd have two angels – one on each shoulder helping me and giving me strength to go on. I'm not a particularly religious person, but I do believe that you get some help and support from those that have passed on.

Coni: I completely agree with you. When we lose loved ones, I believe they become our guides. With Tom's passing, I continue to feel his support. I know he is bringing people into my life and creating opportunities that support this new life that is unfolding.

Ginny: Yes, now my life is so much more fulfilling. Knowing you can help and give back to someone.

Coni: Writing this book and going through the life coach training has put me on a mission. Tom would get upset with me because I worked so much. If we weren't doing something, I was working. Then when he passed, I couldn't go back to that world. I had to move forward.

Ginny: But isn't that interesting? You've gotten off that roller coaster. You're moving forward in a different way.

Coni: Yes, it is an exciting time. Tell me, for people that have lost a child, how did you hold your marriage together? So many people end up getting divorced.

Ginny: Yes, it's a fact that 85% of marriages end in divorce after losing a child, and it doesn't matter if you've lost a child to cancer, or whatever. Kerry and I have been married for 30 some years now.

When Kelty was in first grade and Riley was in kindergarten, my husband and I went through a very hard time. We split up. It was a very important time for me because I learned so much about myself. I've had a lot of loss in my life. I had lost my dad in grade one and my mom in grade four.

My uncle and aunt took us in. They were wonderful people and had adopted two other children previously, but now they had two more and an instant family of six. I was the middle child and didn't think I belonged there. And then there was my Grams. She and I were very close and I could confide in her. She died a couple of months after I got married.

All of these important people in my life had left me, but that was why I couldn't let Kerry in. I didn't know it at the time. I was so scared I was going to lose him too. I now know and understand that but it caused problems in the early years of our marriage. All the losses I had experienced, I honestly think were to prepare me for the loss of my two children.

What's interesting is that Kerry and I are now closer today than we've ever been in our entire lives. We support each other. I'm sure we would have survived but everything happens for a reason. We had to dig deep to understand ourselves. We started learning and having respect for each other.

When Kelty died, I never could have survived without Kerry. He kept me going. When Riley died, we had to be there for each other. We're fortunate that our relationship has grown as it's opposite of what statistics say. Here's why: often people blame the other spouse when a child dies. When Kelty died, I was on a business trip to Florida. Kerry was skiing. Riley was at school. Kelty had come home from Notre Dame and Kerry asked him if he would like to go skiing with him, but Kelty said he would rather stay behind and "study" that fateful day. I know he had this plan and wanted to be in the house by himself. I beat myself up...why didn't I know?

But you can't do that. You have to focus on the things that can make a difference and the things you can control. So now we know there was a potential side effect of the drug Paxil for people under the age of 19. You can have suicidal tendencies the first two weeks after starting to take it. That is what happened to Kelty. He committed suicide within two weeks of taking the first dose.

After his death, my focus was on how to help people and talk about the shame of mental illness. We founded the Kelty Patrick Dehenny Foundation. The foundation provides funds for care, education and research into youth depression-related suicide and other mental illnesses. Our goal is to raise as much money as possible to help those affected by mental illness, especially youth. It's about removing the stigma of this disease and about the conversations and actions that we need to do to make change happen. You have to figure out how to use your energy in a positive way. There's no other choice. It's just something you've got to do.

Coni: Tell me about your bike ride.

23

Ginny: Kerry and I rode our bicycles across Canada to raise money for the Foundation. The goal of *Enough is Enough* was to reduce the stigma associated with mental illness. We rode 109 days from Newfoundland to Whistler. Along the way, we raised money for the education, care and resources required to combat the disease. The ride was a total of 8,000 kilometers or 4971 miles. We raised almost $2 million with this ride.

Coni: Congratulations and how inspiring! Your story is a perfect example of how you can get past the trauma of losing a child. The way you have moved forward is by giving back. I am finding that is a common thread with people that have suffered the loss of a loved one.

Ginny: There are some other things that I know that helped me. When you're thinking, how am I going to get out of bed, how am I going to do that? There is a simple thing, like scheduling something at 9:00 o'clock in the morning.

You really have to push yourself physically so that your mental and emotional health can heal. It's so easy to turn inward and go inside where you ask a lot of questions that can't be answered. I'm a big believer that the physical helps the mental. Yoga or whatever you enjoy. I know for me, if I didn't have that, I don't know where I would be.

Everybody is different but yoga was good for me. That's what Riley did, she was a yoga instructor. After she died, I didn't know what to do. So I went into her studio and put my mat down. Her teacher came out and said, "You know, Riley put her mat down in the exact same place."

Coni: Wow! That gives me goose bumps.

Ginny: That was my place where I could go and connect with her. We just got back from Vancouver and they had given an award in Riley's name. We had a little girl in my yoga class who said she had a birthday party and instead of presents, they were to donate to the charity. She presented me with $367. She had just turned 10. I gave them all t-shirts and put it on the Kelty webpage.

Coni: How many people do you think your foundation has helped?

Ginny: That's a hard question, really hard. I don't know. I know it's a lot but I have no idea. Some of the money is going to the mental health centers, and we want to put the Kelty Patrick Dehenny Foundation in every province of Canada.

****

Ginny's strength and ability to turn grief into positive action is an important part of what we all can do to pull ourselves through the grief process and find the opportunities that are awaiting our discovery. I have said many times that the life I am living now is an exact result of the opportunities that my Crystalline Moments showed me because of Tom's death. It may sound strange that there are opportunities from the loss of a loved one, but indeed Ginny's story underlines that there is opportunity to grow and prosper from the depths of sorrow.

How many times have you heard about someone who has suffered some type of loss and they find a way to give to others because they do not want their loved one's death or illness to be in vain?

It doesn't have to be something as ambitious as raising millions of dollars for mental illness. It can be a simple act of kindness that will make a difference in our sorrow and grief.

Ginny has written an amazing book about her and her husband's journey called *Choosing Hope: A Mother's Story of Love, Loss and Survival*.

To find out more about the foundation and resources for families that are affected by depression and mental illness, go to www.thekeltyfoundation.org.

2 DONNA MIKKIN

When I picked it up, he said, "Donna"...and I grabbed the wall.

Ginny's story shows that we can overcome great grief and find joy in our Crystalline Moments. Her moment occurred when she told the doctor immediately after they had to turn off the life support for Kelty that he was a giver in addition to being an organ donor. He would have wanted to find a way to make a difference.

Other moments happened that she and Kerry both experienced separately and together. The decision to do yoga in Riley's studio and placing her mat in the exact same place that Riley had placed hers is no accident. It gave her a way to connect to her daughter and was an important Crystalline Moment to grow through her sorrow.

Now we turn our attention to how a Crystalline Moment of the exact opposite transpires. I'm sure you have dreamed of winning the lottery. I certainly have and I know what I would do with the money.

We have heard the stories about people who win the lottery, and then a few years later they have lost everything, ending up in worse shape than they were before they won.

The good news is that this story does not end that way, but it is a story about a family winning the New York State Lottery - the second largest jackpot ever won at $34,500,000. What truly happens to your mind and your life when something that huge happens out of-the-blue may surprise you. Donna Mikkin's story is compelling...one of disbelief, happiness, struggle and finding one's footing.

****

Donna and Ed have been together since she was 12 and he was 15 years old. They have since celebrated their 30th wedding anniversary. When you have been with someone that long, there's no need to speak and you just know when there is something going on with each other. Just by breathing a certain way, you know something is up.

In 1990, Donna had started working in real estate. One of the first events she attended was an awards luncheon. She had borrowed a suit to wear because she was a stay-at-home mom and didn't have the appropriate clothes.

She sat and watched people receiving all kinds of awards and then they announced the "Rookie of the Year" award. Up until then, she had politely clapped because it was the right thing to do. The woman who won the award got up to receive it and her husband came out to give her a dozen roses. Donna thought right then and there, "I want that award!" Her desire for the recognition of being Rookie of the Year was a moment of clarity that would create the longing she needed and be a pivotal Crystalline Moment for her.

She was sitting at a table with people she didn't know but informed them that she was going to win that award the following year. She had no idea what she needed to do to earn it, but she declared to everyone that she would be the recipient. She told her manager the next day of her intentions.

He said, "But you don't want to show properties and I can't work with someone that way." So she decided that she would make Rookie of the Year by selling to first-time homebuyers.

It is one thing to put that vision in your mind. It is another thing to put it into action. In her words, "A dream is a dream, but you need to take action." The following year she was Rookie of the Year. We will pick up with her story and our conversation now.

Coni: Tell me about your career before winning the lottery.

Donna: I knew real estate was something I could do. I wanted to contribute to the real estate community. I was in the top 1% of real estate agents in New York State when I became a trainer and a coach. I LOVED doing this work. I worked from my home talking with people who wanted to be better agents for their clients. I was contributing to my family and living in a beautiful home on Long Island.

Coni: So tell me what happened the day you won the lottery.

29

Donna: On February 12, 2007, I was scheduled to talk to a client when my phone rang. It was my husband. When I picked it up, he said, "Donna"...and I grabbed the wall. He's trying to communicate but I'm not listening. I could hear something behind his voice.

When you have lived with someone as long as we have been together, you can read one another's mind. I could tell when he walked into the house whether or not he was in a bad mood. I'm searching in my head, in that moment...what is going on?

He's trying to ground me by saying my name over and over.

"Go to the computer and go to the New York State Lottery site," he said.

"Eddie, cut it out," I demanded. He said it again.

By the time I got to my computer, my hands were shaking so badly I had to cradle the phone under my head. My husband's entire life he's said he is going to win the New York Lottery.

I clicked on the lottery site. "Read me Saturday night's numbers," he said, calmly. So I did.

"Donna, we have all six numbers,' he said. "How much have we won?"

I said, "Eddie, it says there's only one winner. It says $34.5 million dollars!"

"Don't talk to anybody and I'll call you back." Then he hung up!

I'm standing in my living room and I don't know what to do with myself. So I pace and pace and pace. I go running upstairs to my son, Christopher, who was 14 years old. He's playing World of Warcraft on his computer.

"Daddy just called and said we won the lottery," I told him.

He looks at me and goes, "OH!" and returns back to playing his game again. I went downstairs to see where my other son, Eddie Jr. was, who was 18. I called him on his cell phone.

"Mom, what's wrong?" he said, immediately. My son is very connected to me so he instantly knows when something is going on. I told him I needed him to come home alone. No friends.

"I'll be home in a minute," he promised. It takes him 10 minutes and I am wearing a hole in the floor by now. Eddie Jr. pulls into the driveway and opens the front door while I am opening the screen door.

"Daddy won the lottery!" he said to me, knowing.

I called my husband who now is at the lottery office where he had been waiting in line. Just as I called, he had finally gotten up to the front desk where the woman is checking his numbers. They confirmed he was the winner. I told him I needed to talk to him and he handed the phone over to the woman behind the desk.

"Can you tell me this is true?" I asked her.

"Yes," she said. "He's the second largest winner of the New York State Lottery ever."

Eddie gets back on the phone and I asked if I could tell someone.

"Call my mother and sister," he said, "and tell them to come over to the house but don't tell them why."

I hung up the phone but I wasn't thinking clearly. I didn't call them, but jumped into my car to go to my girlfriend Cathy's house. She saw me jump out of the car from inside the house. Now, Cathy's son and my son are best friends. Her immediate reaction was that something was wrong. She came running out while I bolted up the porch stairs. Her husband is behind her.

"What's wrong?" she's yelling. "Are the kids fine?"

"Yes," I yelled back. "We won the lottery!"

Cathy and Frank have been our friends for many years, but her husband said, "I need to talk to Ed first."

Just then Ed called. So Frank grabbed a bottle of wine and he couldn't pour it fast enough. I grabbed the bottle and chugged it. Not that much, but then I went into shock. I heard loud noises...buzzing noises... I was talking and giddy but this buzzing was going on. I told them I needed to line something up and went home.

I called my mother-in-law first. She wanted to know if something was wrong.

"But I can't tell you," I said. "You just need to come right over." You could hear the devastation in her voice.

Then I called my sister-in-law insisting that she had to come over. She kept saying she had to give her daughter a bath. Then she said, "Did you win the lottery?" We both just laughed. Most of the rest of that night was a blur.

The one good thing that happened that first night was that I had always wanted to renew our wedding vows at Disneyland with all of our family and friends there with us. I actually got on the phone that night putting those plans together.

Three months after we won the lottery, we took 40 people to Disneyland. It was the most wonderful magical experience and the culmination of many years of dreams.

Now, what happened to me in the next 24 hours after hearing this news was that my hygiene went out the window! I couldn't comb my hair or take a shower. I would pick up my toothpaste and toothbrush. I knew they went together but I couldn't connect the dots.

Three days later, friends were coming by telling us how happy they were for us. The house looked like a tornado had gone through it. We would just walk around like zombies. Four days later, I was now drinking six bottles of water every 30 minutes.

We called the doctor because I couldn't quench my thirst. "If you don't stop," he said, "you are going to drown." I wasn't allowed to drink any more water - only to have a tablespoon of Gatorade every 15 minutes.

For me, being a commission-based REALTOR®, I understood when you put money in the bank, you could take money out. It never occurred to me that we could just go to the bank and we had money.

My husband felt he was living his destiny. For me, it had never been in my realm of reality that it would ever happen. Everybody sits around a table and talks about what they would do if they won the lottery. Not me. It was never my fantasy.

Coni: What are your earliest memories of those first few days of winning the lottery.

Donna: I would say my earliest memories of the first days after winning the lottery were pure dread. I felt like the hammer was going to drop. If something this good happens, something bad was going to happen. Like the sole survivor of a plane crash.

I really thought, why me? Not my neighbor or someone else. I honestly struggled with that for years. I'm not saying I didn't have joy, but the joy was robbed from me, from feelings of being unworthy and guilty.

It was five years, almost to the day of winning - February 2012 - and I woke up one morning and I said I was going back into real estate. It was as if someone had talked to me in my sleep. I was perfectly clear that I was getting back into real estate. It was definitely a Crystalline Moment. My happiness had been in being a real estate agent and coach. It was my life. I had been taken off the whole plan I had for myself.

For me, the lottery had hijacked the life I was heading toward. I felt out of control in the sense that I was not the person manning the ship anymore. Now I could be a coach and I had the luxury of doing it by design. I wouldn't have any predetermination of financial gain about it. Money was not the reason to go back to work. It was for my self-worth.

Coni: Can you tell me what it was that you experienced when that decision to go back into real estate coaching happened?

Donna: It was that little voice telling me to go back to coaching. I loved coaching. I called a gentleman that I used to train for. He told me that 2012 was not a good year to start a coaching business. Agents didn't have money for anything and coaching had dried up.

However, he agreed to let me attend a training class. There were 75 agents attending the class.

I now ranked in the top 2% of New York real estate agents, so just maybe I knew something about real estate. Also, do you think I could keep my mouth shut if I loved coaching?

So of course, I can't keep my mouth shut and the trainer had to introduce me to everyone. He told the agents about my awards and accolades. At the end of the day, people came up to me and said, "I'll pay you to coach me."

The next day, even more agents wanted coaching. My friend asked me to go to New Jersey for a training class and more agents signed up. The week after that, we go to Chicago and more agents signed up. I can't handle the volume on my own anymore, so now I am hiring coaches. Now I am being asked to be the president of this training company.

I am not working from any kind of fear of loss so the opportunities are flowing to me to live the life of my dreams. All this wonderful business is coming towards me.

Next, I am at a real estate summit and they are talking about hiring speakers. I've never been in a position in my life to witness this. It never would have happened before:

I'm in this room, now president of a training company, and I am watching this speaker on stage. I'm having a Crystalline Moment again. You can get up on the stage and speak to people, it said. It had never occurred to me...all the conventions I had been to in my life watching keynote speakers. The feeling that came over me was exactly the feeling I had when I made Rookie of the Year.

"You mean there is an industry for speakers?" I said to other people there.

They looked at me like I was nuts. I'd gone to the summit in the capacity of a real estate trainer and left knowing what I REALLY wanted to do. Back at my room, I called my husband. I was vibrating, electrified.

"I know what I want to do!" I told him. "I want to be a speaker."

Coni: An amazing story! What did you get from going through all of that?

Donna: What did we get from going through that? It's very much in line with life. That's what resonated when I read your email about Crystalline Moments. There really was an exact moment when I said, "That's my path."

Why didn't I see it before? I've done everything I could to put all the action steps in place to get where I am right now. On Monday, I resigned the real estate training company and on Tuesday, I joined the National Speakers Association.

Then just like a little kid, I was in Indianapolis and called my husband. "I'm a fraud," I told him. "I'm not a speaker."

"This is going to be great for you," he said, but I was not feeling it. When I started in real estate, he had said I was going to be great then too. Sometimes we need someone outside ourselves to see things we don't see in ourselves and can support us on our path. This unworthiness, this belief that we build in our heads wreaks havoc on you.

Coni: What I find interesting is that it took you and your husband winning the lottery for you to find your path.

Donna: Yes, and I am so happy to see where my destiny has brought me. I remember saying out loud that this, being just a lottery winner, is not what I wanted to be. I would never have developed into anything more than what I was before the lottery. I was passionate about coaching people and now it is on such a bigger scale. And that for me is gold.

Coni: I know you are writing a book about your experience. What is the name of it?

Donna: The working title is *The Lottery of Life*.

****

There are several lessons we can take from this part of Donna's story. We do all love to think about what it would be like to win the lottery. How would we handle it? The things that Donna experienced were not a lot different from when something bad happens.

Maybe instead of winning the lottery, you are the sole support for your family and you lose your job. Many of her reactions would be the same had she lost a job. In reality, she lost the work she loved and therefore her life.

Her Crystalline Moment of deciding to go back to real estate could be equated to making the decision to find a new and even better job. Her dream was to get back to helping real estate agents improve their businesses and lives. Now she could do it without the paradigm of worrying about money.

Then Donna's life takes another turn that totally creates the life of her dreams.

One thing that happens when we start finding opportunities in our Crystalline Moments is that we expand and grow into larger and bigger dreams. As a matter of fact, if you know how you are going to reach your goal or dream, then you have not dreamed big enough.

If she and her husband had never won the lottery, she would not be living the life of her destiny. This is the same as what Ginny and I have experienced. If those moments had not happened, we would not be living the lives we have designed for ourselves. You can do the same. Whether you win the lottery, lose a loved one or a job, just by paying attention to the Crystalline Moments and what opportunities are available from them, you can take the steps that will move you forward.

Once you take the first step, then things start happening that you can't explain. A good example of that is when Donna attended the training class in 2012. Real estate agents were hurting badly because of the economy.

But because Donna stepped into her Crystalline Moment and was in alignment with what she was supposed to be doing, she attracted the clients she needed to move forward with her life.

It is important to not only listen to that little voice but to follow where it is leading you, even if you have no idea where you are going to end up. As with Donna, it is not one giant leap but little steps and being open to new opportunities until you get that point of "I know what I want to do" and when you say the words, you vibrate, you feel lighter, electrified...you just know. That is a powerful Crystalline Moment, and one that will lead you to the life of your destiny.

Just like Donna, fears will pop up. Remember that fear is nothing more than a reminder that you are reaching the edge of the life that you have always known. Fear is opportunity.

3 KAREN STOREY

"The only way to go from victim to achiever is to become committed."

One of the most important points of the last two stories is that it doesn't matter whether you are coming from something as tragic as losing your children, or something as incredible as winning a large lottery, the key is to see the opportunities that will arise out of the moment.

Both women stepped into their Crystalline Moment and found the opportunity. We learned that you do it in baby steps. First and foremost, you must recognize and hear the inner voice telling you which direction to go. As you put on and wear that opportunity, additional opportunities will then become available. Those additional moments will lead you to the life you are destined to have.

Ginny and Donna's stories show very supportive families. But what happens with those Crystalline Moments when your family history comes with the blanket of abuse? If you came from an abusive family background, or maybe you are in an abusive relationship now, how can you find your way from abuse to achievement?

The next the two stories are of sisters, Karen Storey and Tricia Andreassen. They found their own Crystalline Moments and moved from being victims to achievers. Both of these women achieved great things and found their way although they started their lives together in a punishing household.

****

As a child, Karen suffered from both physical and sexual abuse. Her first recollection of abuse was around two years of age when her small dog was badly beaten. He laid on the floor not moving and she knew she was next. She ran and hid.

There were some good times but mostly bad times. She moved from abuse as a child to an abusive husband that would not let her out of the house. Her faith in God and believing that someone was standing by her is what got her through her childhood, abusive marriage, loss of a partner and raising a child that was thought to have a learning disability only to find out later her son was gifted.

She protected her younger sister and took care of her so she could be shielded from as much abuse as possible. She then turned her attention to her own children and in particular her son who had difficulties in school. Then when she became a 7th grade teacher, she identified students that were living in abusive situations and does what she can to help them.

Her overall belief is that you can allow yourself to be a victim, or you can have faith in God and trust that there is something better out there for you.

Here is our conversation.

Coni: I am looking forward to our conversation about your life.

Karen: Do you believe in things that can't be explained? Are you a spiritual person?

Coni: Absolutely. Very much so!

Karen: We all go down different paths as we pass through life. Really bad things happen to people. When something bad happens, we become what people say we are and we feel undeserving. Sometimes it happens out of the blue. We were not expecting it and it totally sabotages our lives. When things like that happen, we all go through the feelings of being a victim. We become and feel this because it is beyond our control. We ask questions like, what did I do to deserve this? Or, why wasn't I prepared for this? Everyone has different degrees of victimization that happen to us.

I was eight years old and came home from school. I was a latchkey child. My mom and dad both worked. We lived in a small trailer and when I would get home, I would feed my goldfish. This one day I came home and the goldfish was belly up. I was devastated because the goldfish was my best friend. I told that goldfish everything - all the bad and horrible things that happened - everything. It was the only confidant I had and I was used to talking to it to think things through. Then I remembered

43

the story of how Christ told Naaman to go to the river and dunk seven times to wash away his sins.

I dunked my goldfish and prayed, and then I dunked him again and prayed. I sobbed the whole time. I don't know if I gave him mouth-to-mouth or what but he came back to life. He swam around and lived for several days. At that point, for the first time, I felt like someone was listening and heard my prayers. Somebody cared about what I was going through. I have always had the feeling that someone was with me, always walking behind me, but this was the first time I recognized it.

While in college, I didn't have enough money to go back to school. I prayed and someone spoke to me but nobody was there. This voice said, "Karen, you will never need or want or lack for anything. Just trust me."

Coni: And did you trust?

Karen: Yes, why wouldn't I? Where did I have to go? When you've reached the bottom of the barrel and you're still feeling victimized in every possible way...when you have nothing. You don't even own your body, but you still have your mind. That is the place you can go to. When that is all you own because someone has taken control of everything you have, what choice do you have but to trust?

I remember when I was 14 and facing my own mortality. I was deciding that day whether I was going to live or die. You know what kept me alive? My baby sister, Trish! I picked *my life*. I had to make sure that she was going to be okay. That whatever was in my strength, in my power, in my life, my breath and my spirit, I would make sure she would be okay.

44

I graduated high school and went to college at age 15. I thought, okay, all that stuff was behind me. When you want to start over again and you want to put all the bad things behind you, you roll them all up in a little ball and toss the ball back there in that old life. You think, I don't have to worry about this anymore, but it doesn't work that way. It comes back in different cycles and different ways. That is why when I got married the first time, I went back into an abusive relationship. I had not dealt with all the baggage.

I was working three jobs while in college. For me, I knew if you don't work, you don't eat. At 16, I was the resident dorm supervisor. I was a lab assistant and waited tables. I went through my freshman year and worked all summer to save money. I went back to school and when I got ready to leave at Christmas, they told me I would not be able to come back because I owed too much money. Now what was I going to do?

I decided to write President Ford a letter. What did I have to lose? I wrote that I was trying with everything in me to go to school but I didn't have the money. I wrote the letter in my own handwriting and then thought, well he isn't going to believe me unless I put a picture in there. So I was 17 and sent the letter probably signed, 'Love Karen' along with my picture. Some time passed...maybe it was January or February, and I got this phone call. It was the president of the college. President Ford had sent his representative on my behalf to get me back in school!

Coni: So were you able to go back to school?

Karen: I went back to school but then got married and had children. The marriage was a very bad decision. I was working trying to take care of my family when a friend got me a job at Owen Mill Majestic as a telemarketer. I started winning

45

prizes and trips just talking to people. It was so much fun that it gave me a rush! It gave me a great break from the really terrible things that were happening in my home life.

My friend who was my supervisor decided to go out on his own and start his own company called Monarch Photographics. There were four of us that came together to birth the company. It was great because I could work at home, take care of my children and do whatever I needed to do. We were supposed to go to a convention in Kansas City and my favorite partner said he didn't think he would be able to make the trip because he really wasn't feeling well. I said no worries, we'll handle it. On the way back from the convention, I stopped at a pay phone and called him. They didn't have cell phones in those days. The doctors weren't sure what was wrong with him so they were sending him to Birmingham, Alabama for tests. It turns out he had acute leukemia. After a period of time, with many tests and attempts to save his life, he died. He died twelve days after my divorce. He had been not just a partner, but a best friend.

Coni: How long were you married to your abusive husband?

Karen: Six years, four months and so many days.

Coni: So with everything you went through as a child, then being married to an abusive husband, were you like so many other people who feel like they deserve the abuse? Or, did you feel you just needed to get through it?

Karen: I felt I needed to push through it. Having an analytical or scientific mind, I would try to figure out where the disconnect was. I never felt that I deserved it, however, I had two children so I didn't know how to step away from it either. I tried

46

to be the peacemaker, the appeaser. Brought up by a preacher and being in that ministerial environment, how did you get a divorce? If you do, you will go straight to hell so you try to work through it.

The deciding moment for me, when I decided I needed to get out of the marriage no matter what, was when my husband kicked my son's front teeth out. He had turned his rage to me and kicked. My son just happened to be in the way. That was a defining moment. I was like, 'NO, OH NO, that's not going to happen!' That night I laid there and thought about how I was going to kill him. I decided that was probably not the best choice because then who was going to raise my children. I didn't trust anyone else.

For the next several days, I kept this little tiny travel bag hidden. Then one day I had this window of opportunity. I grabbed the kids and I ran. My uncle was Chief of Police of this little town in West Virginia. I went to him and told him what was happening. He contacted the Chief of Police in my town in Tennessee. We went into hiding. At this point, I was also in the process of losing my home. Thank goodness I had some friends in real estate so they assumed my loan. They gave me $3000 and since I was still in hiding, my uncle transferred and handled everything. I finally came back to Tennessee with a police escort.

My son can still remember me taking knives and jamming them around the doors to keep us safe. Just before my partner died, he called and said that he had talked to the attorney and had taken care of everything for me and my kids. We would be okay. After he died, the paperwork never materialized. I never got anything from the business.

Here I was with a 15 month-old and a 4 year-old, no money, no business, no home and in hiding. I went back to the little town where my parents were living and moved into a little trailer. I went on food stamps and to the Methodist Church every week for a bag of groceries - the most humiliating time of my life. I had no other way to feed my children though. I asked God what I was supposed to do now. I got this idea that I was supposed to go back to school.

I went to the Registrar at Virginia Tech who said they would talk to their attorneys to see if tuition could be granted for me. I got a Fulbright scholarship, all expenses paid and basically a free education as long as I went to school to be a teacher. Now the kids could be with me in the school system. I wouldn't need child care.

My son was diagnosed as learning disabled and was having trouble with social skills. No wonder, right? At 18 months old, he was under my kitchen table with a screwdriver unscrewing the legs off the table. He walked at 4 ½ months in his walker with a juice cup. I didn't know that meant he was gifted.

I graduated from Virginia Tech magna cum laude. I continued on to get my master's degree. My son was in the second grade and going through issues at school. I went to my advisor who helped me get the help my son needed. When I started teaching, they said I should find a gifted child to work with.

You know how they separate kids that can't keep up and put them in a trailer behind the school? That was where my son was. I went to his school and insisted that he get tested as gifted. It turns out he was highly gifted.

This allowed me to work with my son. When he got older, he ended up attending the Air Force Academy. When he performed his endurance runs, they found out he had a heart condition and discharged him. He lost his dream.

He ended up going to Emory University with a friend of his, graduating with honors. He wanted to become a chiropractor. He started a special international project...something that would help the handicapped. While working on the project, he downloaded thousands of files.

Unfortunately, he downloaded a file that had been flagged by the FBI. Since the file was tagged, he heard a knock on the door and they arrested him. Because it crossed international lines, he spent a year in state prison then transferred to federal. I had to go to court when they were moving him.

At first, I went by myself and felt so alone. I said, "I can't do this!" My baby sister, Trish, said she would come with me. It was a gift because we went through everything together. This was such a very difficult time.

One day while we were at the courthouse, Trish went to put money in the parking meter and instantly had a song come to mind. She called it, Walk in Faith. Later, she recorded the song on a CD for me and with that song, I prayed and prayed. I then remembered the voice that told me that I would never need or want for anything. I wrote that on a piece of paper and stuck it on my mirror so I would see it every day.

Coni: So what do you think helped you through all of this?

Karen: I have a choice every day. Everyone has a choice every day. When we start the day and we're being victimized, how do we get through it? We get through it by talking and listening to others that are inspiring, or reading something that is inspiring. We can speak to our higher power and by believing that someone out there cares. THAT is how you get through it.

Whatever happens today is just for this day but that does not mean it is your destiny. That's what is in this moment. The journey is greater. It is a path and all along the way, there are people we are supposed to love, cherish and inspire. We are meant to be their cheerleader. That's when you become a victor instead of a victim.

When you quit being angry and say, "That's done!" When you get through that, you're a champion. That is why I am a teacher. If I can impact one life every year, that's what my life is about. Opportunities come all the time. We can choose to live in fear—fear is just anger turned inside out—or we can choose to live life.

We either choose to live life as a victim or not. It's your choice whether you want to play that role. We get stuck in things and it doesn't start as adults. It starts when we are children.

Kids that experience poverty and abuse don't know any different and most likely they're parents don't know any different. The question is how to break that cycle...a critical question.

Coni: How do you break the cycle because it can be many generations that this has been happening?

50

Karen: You weave in and out of it, moving from being a victim to a survivor. You hang on, you hold out, you get along, you get by, you subsist, you thrive, then you prevail. It's why some people move forward and others get stuck. Defining Crystalline Moments happens throughout our lives.

When you feel like a victim, there is a physical point of progression and you get to the point where you can say you are surviving. You are hanging on and want to persist. You begin to feed those pieces. Each tiny piece of persistence will provide tiny baby steps that will help build your commitment to a different life.

When you come through that, you become an achiever. The only way to come from being a victim to being an achiever is to become committed. You must follow through, prevail, negotiate, compete, complete and finish whatever passage you are on. If at any point you can't push through, you stay a survivor.

****

Karen's story outlines how the love for a younger sister saved the life of the older sister. Many siblings can relate to taking care of one another whether due to abuse, neglect or illness. Millions of children and young adults in our world only have each other to depend on. They too can benefit from their Crystalline Moments.

Tricia's life may have been completely different if Karen, at the age of 14, had made a different choice. Instead of ending her life, she chose to protect Tricia from what she was going through.

Hers is also a story of both difficult and rewarding Crystalline Moments. We all have that inner voice and Karen heard hers loud and clear..."Karen, you will never need or want or lack for anything. Just trust me."

Karen's ability to push through and see the potential while going through horrific events was extraordinary. She defines what having a Crystalline Moment and finding the opportunity means.

Her message of going from victim to survivor to achiever can be used in anyone's story that feels they have been a victim. At one time or another, we all have thoughts of being victimized. The bottom line is commitment or as she would say, pushing through it is what creates achievers.

Without commitment, our life's dream will not prevail. Without Crystalline Moments, the direction or opportunities of our lives would not show themselves.

4 TRICIA ANDREASSEN

"You need to recognize them when they happen and know that it's the Universe speaking to you."

A recurring theme from Karen's story and the others is that moving forward is done by putting one foot in front of the other. We don't just go from abuse to being a successful happy person in one big step. We take "baby" Crystalline Moment steps.

Tricia Andreassen is the baby sister Karen mentioned in her story. The gift Karen gave to Tricia was the possibility for Tricia to grow and achieve.

Tricia is now married to the love of her life and has an amazing son, Jordon. She went through a difficult time of her own when her first husband cheated on her at the same time she miscarried their first child. We will talk later about her 'moments' while going through that time in her life. But now we're going to lighten it up a bit. Tricia has a wonderful fun story centered around Crystalline Moments while working on her novel. In this conversation, we are not going to discuss Tricia's childhood. We'll start where Tricia is today.

I met Tricia just three weeks after my husband passed away when I attended a conference I have now been going to for seven years called AFIRE, an acronym for Awesome Females in Real Estate.

That year, Bernice Ross, the founder of AFIRE, had personally invited me to come as her guest if I thought it would help in my healing process.

I had not met Tricia before but she came up and introduced herself, giving me a big hug. I immediately felt a bond to her. She had written a song about what AFIRE meant to her and when she sang it, I felt surrounded by angels. She and the other AFIRE ladies who supported me played a big part in my healing journey.

Tricia is a very successful businesswoman and owns four companies. One of them, ProStep Marketing and Advertising, offers tools and support to business owners to help them with their advertising and marketing needs. She speaks at the National Association of REALTORS® and other regional meetings of real estate associations and large franchise annual meetings.

She is a successful executive coach commanding top dollar for her abilities. Her book, *Interfusion Marketing*, is a #1 bestseller with rave reviews.

But we are not going to discuss Tricia, the businesswoman either.

Tricia has a whole other side to her. She also is one of the most artistic people I have ever met. In addition to being a successful bestselling business author, she is also a songwriter, artist and working on a wonderful novel. This novel is truly her passion.

Her story centers around how the opportunities develop when you are in alignment with your passion. It also shows how you move forward to have an amazing life when forced to start over.

****

Coni: I remember the day you called me all excited about this painting you had discovered, and how it fit into your novel. I remember you called to tell me, "I just had a Crystalline Moment! I have to tell you about it!" What inspired you to write this novel, and what was inspiring about the painting? Why was it a Crystalline Moment?

Tricia: The last few years, I've been going to a place called Jekyll Island, a barrier island off the coast of Georgia. The island is like heaven; very quiet and 65% of the land is undeveloped. There are no chain stores or restaurants anywhere on the island.

I am completely drawn to its beauty and peacefulness. Because of that, I started writing my novel using Jekyll Island as the backdrop. I don't know where the book came from, but it just started spilling out of my head and heart.

I am writing about a character who became an artist after his wife died. He had discovered his muse and started painting. One of the chapters talks about the paintings the character had dropped off at a local art gallery on the island. In the book, I describe one of the paintings as a picture of a turtle coming out of the ocean and coming onshore to nest.

Jekyll Island is a protected area for turtle nesting. There were 192 turtle nests created last year. I describe the turtle in the painting as having three-fourths of its body out of the wake. She is coming out of the ocean to lay her nest. She's lit up by moonlight which has lit up the entire sky. I describe the scene in great detail in my book.

You know how life takes a turn and you never know what opportunities lay before you? It is amazing! My husband and I decided to make a trip to Jekyll, just a little romantic getaway for us. I decided to go to the small village on the island to visit some of the shops.

The village is in my book and has inspired some of the story. It has quaint shops and I walked into one that inspired me which I featured in my book. I was talking to the owner about my book and she told me about this art gallery. She said the gallery featured local artists.

That was weird, I thought. I talked about a shop that featured local artists in my book. I go to the gallery and I am walking around with Ann, who works there. She is explaining some of the local art. We head upstairs and I walk around a corner and there it is, a picture on an easel. It was EXACTLY the description of the painting in my book!

I actually got chills! It was kind of frightening and I kept going back and looking at it. I kept saying to myself I should buy it, but I left and went to another store.

Coni: I remember you called and talked to me about buying it.

Tricia: Well, I ended up coming back and buying the painting. I spoke with Ann about the artist. I told her this painting was done for me to find.

She said it was a one-of-a-kind original painted by a local artist. There were no other reproductions. I told her my story. She was completely amazed. "I'll give you the name and number of the artist so you can talk to him," she said.

I called the artist and he explained that when he started the painting, it was inspired by his mom, the same thing I explained in my book. He said that when the economy got real bad, he was looking for extra money. He told his wife that maybe he could sell some paintings to relieve them of the economic hard times. He went to a Hobby Lobby store to buy all the paint and supplies. In less than a year, he was making 50% of his income from his paintings.

Before I bought the painting, I had called Ann at the gallery and told her about the chapter in my book where my character came into a gallery and dropped off five paintings. She called me back leaving a voice mail. "Tricia, I called the shop owner and guess what? The artist had brought five paintings to the shop the day he dropped this painting off."

When I heard that message, I rushed back to the shop. Ann said that she knew this was going to sound weird, and a lot of people bring in their personal stories to the gallery, but she could feel the Holy Spirit around this story. I had goose bumps and could not control them.

Coni: This story blew me away. I completely believe we can create our own reality and this is a beautiful example of that. I remember when you called me to tell me what was happening, that it was pouring down rain and even though it was nasty outside, you were compelled to go to the shops.

Tricia: Yes, it was not just a rain storm. It was tropical storm Andrea. I decided no matter what I had to go to the shop. When I went out, it was raining sideways.

Coni: Do you believe everything happens for a reason?

Tricia: Yes, I believe that everything happens to us for a reason. Even in tragedy and sadness. Something develops around that.

When I was 26 years old, I was married to my first husband and went through a miscarriage. I didn't know until the day I had the ultrasound that my baby had not developed. It was already dead. You know how excited you are when you go to your ultrasound. It is the first time you are going to see your baby and all the excitement of bringing a new life into the world. Not my experience. The following night, I ended up going through a pretty terrible miscarriage. I was in the hospital, completely distraught, and I just remember crying. I had always wanted a child and to be a mom.

Within a year of having the miscarriage, I went through a divorce. My husband had an affair and I caught him. I had to start all over. I'm now 42 and have used all the emotions and feelings

I had back then to put into the character in my book. The story and inspiration now come from a whole different channel.

So out of tragedy comes a beautiful story. I believe our faith, our spirituality, the Universe are like our flowers to bloom. It just comes from inside of you. That is when the opportunities need to be recognized and celebrated from those Crystalline Moments. You need to recognize them when they happen and know that it's the Universe speaking to you.

Coni: You said it beautifully. That is exactly what this book is all about. I really believe if you come with an open heart, you will recognize the moments and the opportunities that arise out of those moments.

****

Tricia's is a wonderful story of how the clarity of your imagination and thoughts create a reality. The Crystalline Moment that happened when she wrote the chapter in the book created the painting that appears in the shop.

When you look into the teachings of the new thought leaders and books like *The Secret*, they talk about how, if you align your energy with what you are put on this earth to do, you will live the life of your dreams. If you can envision your dream and come through your paradigms, you will have the life you want to live.

Tricia's story about the character in her book and the artist that actually created the painting are no accident. If she had not had a miscarriage and gone through a divorce, her character would not have had the same emotions nor would it have created the connection between Tricia and the real artist.

Tricia is now an amazing artist on her own and has sold her own paintings. She has a beautiful catalog of inspirational songs and her book, *Interfusion Marketing*, can be found on Amazon.com.

What is even more amazing about this story is that now Tricia has paintings in the same art gallery where she bought her turtle painting. Talk about full circle Crystalline Moments!

This is all because of the love of a big sister who chose life over death. Now that gives *me* goose bumps!

5 KENZIE WILLIAMS

"So when an idea comes, don't just think of everything and not do anything..."

In Tricia's conversation, she talks about not knowing where her book was coming from. We have all heard about artists and musicians where the painting or song just comes to them, or sometimes in dreams.

Tricia's artistic endeavors are all like that. In the conversation with her sister, Karen talks about Tricia walking to put money in the parking meter and coming back with a song she entitled, "Walk in Faith". A song she thought of and sang to give her sister hope.

Those inspirations are the Universe providing us with a Crystalline Moment that if we don't recognize and act on the opportunity, will be gone or will affect our life as we move forward. It is so important to see the opportunity as soon as it arrives.

As children, we see things without the prism of fear or doubt. My next conversation is one that is very near and dear to my heart. It is a conversation I did with my granddaughter, Kenzie. Now you may be thinking, oh no! Now she's going to pull out pictures of her grandkids. Well, I am not above that! But I think you will understand why I had this conversation with Kenzie for this book when you're finished reading her story.

As of this writing, Kenzie is now a teenager and just turned 13 years old. Her story starts when she was just eight years old.

****

Kenzie is very much a girlie girl. She loves bling and was very much a princess while she was growing up. Kenzie is not a plain blue jean kind of girl and forget about t-shirts. She always has had an eye for dressing with flair. Even when she was very tiny, she knew what she wanted. I remember my daughter-in-law, Molly, telling me one time when I suggested that I would like to take Kenzie shopping for her birthday, that it was not a good idea. She informed me that taking Kenzie shopping was an event not for the faint of heart.

Here is our intimate conversation.

****

Coni: I wanted to write about you and Taylor (my other granddaughter) because you both have become amazing human beings that have done so much already in your very short lives.

You both started at a very young age to create the lives of your dreams. When I was 10, I had Crystalline Moments that have affected my life for the last 55 years. I want to show people how they need to look at their own childhood and those of their children and see the opportunities that are available when Crystalline Moments happen many times when we are children. How old were you when you decided you wanted to sew?

Kenzie: I think I was seven, but I was eight when I actually started to sew. I started just doing hems and things, then I started on the machine. I had a lot of fun using the sewing machine.

Coni: Was sewing and fashion design something that you had to think about, or was it something that was just there?

Kenzie: I really didn't think about it. I didn't know much about the whole other world behind the scenes of fashion designing because it's not really talked about that much. But I loved sewing and wanted to know more.

Coni: I explained the Crystalline Moments that I had as a child. Can you recall any moments as they apply to your designs?

Kenzie: I don't recall exactly when it started, but I was trying to fall asleep and had a headache that day and a picture popped into my head. Now that is when designs pop into my head. The first time it happened, I was thinking of being in a garden with my family. I later drew a picture of it and my dress kept changing in my mind. Those were my first three designs. That was in 2010 so I was nine.

Coni: So now you see pictures of fashion designs in your head? They just come to you? That's like a musician or artist when they have songs or art pieces that just appear in their head.

Kenzie: Yes, it can be annoying because I am trying to go to sleep and I get these fashion designs popping into my head. I don't want to have to get up and draw them all out but they are going around in my head. It only happens when I have a headache and I am trying to go to sleep.

Coni: I just met this woman who studies brains and she said headaches sometimes are a sign of ideas trying to come out.

Kenzie: I will go for a while without having any designs come to mind. It comes and goes. Sometimes I get worried that it won't happen again but then it comes back. I am just thankful that the designs keep coming. The first time, I drew out the three designs and got some fabric, but ended up not actually making them. I started thinking about fashion shows and fashion designers. I also started thinking of private jets and the fashion world. So then I wanted to start actually working on it. This is not something that is going to happen in a year or two. I am going to have to really want it to be successful.

Coni: That is a sign of a true artist, you know. What about fashion design do you like most? Do you like the drawing of the designs or the sewing of the designs? Is there one part of the process that you like better than another?

Kenzie: I really like the final piece. What's funny is that it never looks like the design you draw. It's always a little different.

Coni: After the young gal who was from Paris and was a fashion journalist came to stay with me, I had asked her to reach out to you. She had recommended a school called St. Martin's in London that has a great fashion design program. When I told you what she said, you told me that you had already checked it out. How old were you when you started checking out schools for fashion design?

Kenzie: Back when I was eight, I thought I wanted to go to Oxford and I still might like to, but that's not really a design school. I don't really want to go to design school because I feel with what I want to do, business school is more useful. I started checking out design schools around my 11th birthday, but soon after decided I wanted to go to a business school. I'm now thinking Berkeley because it has a small design program but it is a high-level program. But that could change.

Coni: You stay very busy designing and then actually sewing your designs. Between that and school, you don't have a lot of time for friends. Do you feel like you are missing out or sacrificing other parts of your life?

Kenzie: I don't really think about it. I don't feel like I am sacrificing. There have been times when my friends have wanted me to come over and I actually didn't want to. I wanted to work on my designs. That was kind of hard. The other thing I have said is I am not going to have another sleepover until I finish a design I am working on. You need friends and they are important, but when you have part of your life that is an adult life, you then have responsibilities that go along with that.

Coni: So if there is a young person out there that has these things popping into their head, whether it is fashion design or building cars, do you have any advice on how to get them from an idea to whatever they want to create? Any advice on actions that can make that happen?

Kenzie: My suggestion is getting something out on paper, start thinking it through because that is when you will start to see all the other steps you need to take. So when an idea comes, don't just think of everything and not do anything. Just start working on it...even if you don't know where the ideas are going. Then you will be able to figure out, do I want to do this or do I not want to do this?

Coni: That is great advice. Now what kind of advice would you give to parents that have a child that is having things pop into their head?

Kenzie: Don't doubt them. If it is not a good idea, tell them, but if it is a good idea, help them but it needs to be what they want. Don't push them because it is something you want for them. Don't change around things they are doing. Let them learn and do it on their own. Just let them be themselves. It has to be their own idea and the parents just need to make sure their child is happy. That is the most important thing.

****

Kenzie knows exactly where she wants to go. Her Crystalline Moments come in the form of headaches that then become fashion designs. She is a great example of not ignoring those moments and how to take charge and do something with them.

She has a picture of the plane and the home she is going to own. She sees herself as a famous fashion designer and has the tenacity and drive to make it happen. She is a perfect example of someone living their dream and making it happen.

We can never "get to" our dreams. We must live from our dreams then take steps to close the gap from where we are and the vision of our life. We do not need to know or understand how it is going to happen. We just must be at the frequency and alignment of our dream.

Kenzie sees and acts like she is already a successful designer. And the great news is, at 13, she is a great designer. She has even designed a dress for a young movie actress to wear on the red carpet for a movie premiere. Not bad!!

Her parents told her after she finished six design pieces, they would help her get a website. She designed the website and runs her business with very little help from Mom and Dad. As a matter of fact, her mom says she now goes to Kenzie when she wants an idea on how to sew something.

Kenzie gave some very good advice for all of us: when we have an idea pop into our head, we need to nurture it to see where it is going to go. Try it on and see how it feels. If it is a child, we want to encourage those moments but not influence them so much that it becomes our idea instead of their own.

Kenzie's parents will help when asked but unless it is something major, they will allow Kenzie to learn on her own and make her own mistakes. Thomas Edison, after failing 10,000 times to invent the lightbulb, would tell people it was not 10,000 failures, just 10,000 ways that didn't work.

Albert Einstein said, "Anyone who has never made a mistake has never tried anything new." The best thing we can do for our children is allow them to learn and that includes making mistakes.

Kenzie has designed clothing for herself, family and friends. She has sold several pieces, including the one I mentioned for the movie actress. She attended the NXT Fashion Week in Portland at age 12 and was asked by a designer to come back to the VIP event the next night.

She has been invited to visit Los Angeles by some of the designers there to work with their team.

More personally, she designed the formal wear for her and her sister on a cruise the family was taking.

You can check out Kenzie's designs on her website at www.kkcouturefashion.com.

6 ROB CHRANES

"Then suddenly, the company I was working for went bankrupt. I was out of a job..."

Eight hundred years ago there was a Persian poet named Rumi. In one of his quotes, he said, "It's as if a king has sent you into a far and distant land with one specific task to accomplish. You could accomplish a hundred other things, but if you fail to accomplish the one thing for which you've been sent to do, in the end, it will be as if you accomplished nothing."

When we are young like Kenzie, many of us have no idea what we are going to do when we grow up. Some of us go through life still searching for that 'thing' that we are put here to do. I have friends in their 60's and 70's still asking what they want to be when they grow up. We are never too old to find our purpose and passion.

Some of us allow the Universe to direct the pages of our lives rather than writing our own story. As we become adults, we have conditions and circumstances that start to dictate our lives and that is where we get stuck. Wouldn't it be wonderful if we all understood what Kenzie knows instinctively?

Not all of us have headaches that bring on inspiration. Sometimes it takes time for our true passion to emerge. We do all kinds of other things just like Rumi suggests. Many of us ignore the signs. Sooner or later, after a few pebbles, stones and brick walls we will have the opportunity to move into our vision of our own life. The only thing stopping us is our fear and conditions.

Rob is a good example of trying different things and having Crystalline Moments along the way that helped guide him to his dream. Rob's story emphasizes that when we are being shown what we are supposed to be doing, we need to step into it with faith and belief.

The one thing that Kenzie knows that Rob had to find out is that without commitment to your dream, it doesn't matter how talented you are.

You can have the longing, but if you are not willing to do the work and follow the steps to bridge the gap to your dream, then that dream will not happen.

****

Coni: How old were you when you were working as a band road manager?

Rob: I was 22. That was the first time I can say I had a Crystalline Moment. As a band manager, I recognized that it took more than talent in this world to succeed. Musicians need to be committed and willing to do the work if they want to become a great band. You can apply that to everything you do in life.

That was the point when I decided I needed to change course. I needed to settle down so I decided I needed to go to school. However, even though I knew that was what I needed to do, I also found out that I had to do the work. I ended up leaving college and taking low paying jobs.

About a year after I quit college, I needed some surgery which required a lengthy recuperation time. I had an opportunity to read a lot. I read a fiction book that was about this guy who lived on the Greek Isles. I thought I would like to make some money so I could live like that.

In order to make money, I figured I needed to become some kind of professional. But how am I going to find a profession? This discomfort crept up on me. I kept pushing it back but it kept coming up. Since I never finished college, how was I ever going to become a professional?

I went to my parents' house and was reading the job ads. I finally asked my father, "All week long I see young people in Atlanta. They are driving nice cars and having a good time. What do you think they do?"

"Oh, they are probably in real estate or banking," he said. He told me about when they bought their house, the statement showed that the real estate agent made 6% of the purchase price.

My moment of clarity! I figured out on a $100,000 house that I would not have to sell very many houses in a year to live well. Of course, I'm not thinking or even aware of commission splits, expenses and what the competition is like.

That's how I started on a real estate career path. I did that for 14 years; as an agent listing and selling properties. Totally, in hindsight, it was unrealistic and idiotic on my part. When I started selling real estate, I was 23 years old, unmarried, I had no experience buying and selling homes. And I had only been in Atlanta for a very short time so I didn't have a network of contacts. So I struggled trying to learn the business. I didn't know how much I didn't know about real estate and didn't know in the beginning how to build a successful career.

Also, in 1974, it was a horrible real estate market. I struggled along working for a very large company. Then I switched and went to work for a much smaller company where I would have an opportunity to become a manager sooner. The company I went to work for was owned by a husband and wife team who had a vision to grow the company. It was a much better fit for me.

Another Crystalline Moment happened when I transitioned from the real estate business to the mortgage business. There was a guy in the mortgage business that was in my real estate office. He told me that he thought I needed a change. He said I could tell him to mind his own business, but he recognized that after 14 years of real estate sales, I needed something different to give me something fresh to do.

He saw that in me before I saw it in myself. He planted the seed and I gave it some thought for about two months. I decided to jump into the mortgage business. It opened my eyes. It was one of those things that felt like it was the right thing at the right time.

I was in the mortgage business for 20 years, starting out as a loan originator then I moved into sales management and other senior leadership positions.

Once again, sometimes things just fall neatly in place. That is what happened when I decided I should work for a different company. There was a person who was the legal counsel for my company and he decided to leave and go into a joint venture with one of the banks in town to start a new mortgage company.

You sense you are going in the right direction when things start falling into place and the opportunities from those Crystalline Moments present themselves. It was almost effortless.

I spent 12 years there until suddenly I found myself unemployed. About six months before I became unemployed, I had this idea for a new business that was just starting to germinate.

Coni: How did the idea come to you?

Rob: I remember that moment like it was yesterday. I had bumped into down payment assistance programs over the years in both real estate and mortgage. I would try to encourage different programs based upon how it would increase the number of loans that could be made if some kind of a down payment program could be made available.

I would have ideas on how to make a down payment assistance program work. One time, I put out an email to talk about how to use this type of program to train young recruits and increase loans. At that time, the bank had an award called LEND that stood for Leadership Excellence in Neighborhood Development. I won the award that year, not completely because of that email, but they knew I was trying. I was one of 115 out of 60,000 employees that won.

The seeds, the frustration and challenges were planted then. It wasn't until toward the end of my time with that bank that it came home again that this type of program was needed.

There was a development company that brought us in to be a lender for one of their projects. The project sat in a tax allocation district and one of the conditions of the allocation was that it had to be planned with 25% of affordable units. The developer told us they would allow us to be an approved lender for just the affordable part.

I was the loan officer responsible for managing that account and getting loan officers involved. It was around a year before I developed a specific plan of what was needed for the project. All of this was leading up to the moment when I would get some clarity on how to be successful in working with clients for our portion of the project.

I was a member of an organization that was made up of primarily real estate developers. A man presented the organization with a $5,000,000 gift for what they were calling a workforce housing center. A lot of the things that were a part of the organization really didn't relate to me, however, now they are getting into an area where I had some expertise. I was familiar with the ownership side, so I got onto the steering committee for the pilot program for the workforce housing center.

The first thing I imagined when I heard workforce housing center was a one-stop shop. A place where developers, commercial or residential builder lenders could go and find out about all the loan and down payment assistance programs that were available to them..

Most counties or communities have incentives that can be used for revitalization of areas. Tax breaks and other assistance programs are available. There is just a massive amount of information and rules that contradict each other to navigate through these programs. I envisioned the center being manned by people that were familiar with the different programs so that people who didn't do this every day could come and get answers.

From there, I narrowed down my scope a little bit. I asked the question, isn't anyone aggregating all of this information and organizing it into a simple database? It seemed like the time to do it and I couldn't believe it hadn't been done. The seed is now germinated and the concept is starting to grow.

Then suddenly, the company I was working for went bankrupt. I was out of a job.

My first reaction was I started looking for another job but I had the luxury, the motivation and the reality of the marketplace that all came together to slow me down and let me take my time. I had a three-month period of time that allowed me to get out of the routine and get the blinders off. I could slow down my thinking and expectations.

A former real estate coach I had worked with put me in touch with others in her company. They were very helpful and provided me with exercises. One exercise was, if you could do anything, what would you do? Then you wrote a job description. That whole combination of events helped me expand my imagination.

That is when I started testing my idea out on some people in the business. Pretty quickly, I was getting positive feedback. That was in 2007. In December of that year, I started writing a rough draft of the business plan.

In January, my wife asked, "Are you going to pursue this or are you going to get a job?" We talked about how we could tighten our belts. My daughter from a previous marriage was grown, so the climate was favorable to pursue this.

We decided to give it all of 2008 and see if it went anywhere and re-evaluate at the end of the year. My dream would provide a one-stop shop for down payment assistance programs that are available in all the different areas around the country.

Coni: You're very good at listening to your instincts and inner guidance.

Rob: Maybe it's my nature and my experience. It could be like the saying, "necessity is the mother of invention". With the zigzag direction I have taken in my life, I think I needed to get creative in how I thought about things. When things don't feel comfortable or right, you have to think about it and make changes.

Coni: There are a lot of people who have a dream but they don't act on it. When you discussed things with your wife about this new venture and decided to give it a year, how did you start and what would be a piece of advice that you would give to someone that has a dream?

Rob: Just start doing your homework. Learn all you can about it. Talk to people and then start testing the dream. You need to get your mindset out of the status quo in terms of what you can afford to do and what you can't.

You can have the best idea in the world but you need to make arrangements to give it the time it needs to turn from a seed to seedling. You have to *make* it happen. For me, I had to take my blinders off. It took a few months of me getting out of my routine and being out of the business for my eyes to open.

Another important thing is that if you can add value to someone else, you can't miss. I couldn't do something that didn't have a purposeful role. Being able to help people with down payments for their dream homes is very rewarding.

Everybody has awoke from a dream and not been able to remember the specifics but still be disappointed because it was just a dream. That's what it feels like to me...this is a dream. But this is my dream and it's real. I'm living it.

Coni: What was the biggest help in launching your dream?

Rob: My real estate coach and her company were a huge influence on me. They were mortgage experts but before we created anything in the mortgage area, the first exercise I had to do was create a life plan. I was like, can we do this later? And they said, no!

Your life, your career, your relationships are all intertwined. You can't have one without the other being in harmony. A lot of that coaching over the years helped open my mind and look at my work and what the purpose was behind it.

Coni: That explains a lot then. Having to look at your life and what you are aspiring to have in your life has everything to do with why you are living your dream now. How long did you work with a coach?

Rob: I want to say about four years. I still talk to my coach on a fairly regular basis. We stay in touch with one another. I appreciate why you are excited to be writing this book and being a Life Mastery Consultant. The kind of impact this book and your coaching will have on people's lives will be incredibly fulfilling.

Coni: It is nice to talk to someone who has worked with a coach and to see how you are doing now. You are proof that coaching can make a significant difference in your life.

Rob: Yes, you're right. It's a phenomenal feeling and peace of mind that comes with it. You just keep saying you are going to go where your next dream takes you. To me, it's like stepping on a magic carpet.

Coni: Yeah, I have that same feeling when I talk about my life plans. It's like I'm floating!

Rob: Yeah, it's an extraordinary experience that I feel many times a day.

****

Rob talks about being a band road manager and realizing that it takes more than talent to be successful. It takes commitment. In any Crystalline Moment, we have opportunity but if we are not willing to do the work, then that opportunity will be gone.

He also talks about the Crystalline Moment when he decided he wants to be a professional but without a college degree, what could he do. The longing was there but it was the discontent that kept welling up in him that gave him the clarity he needed to start looking into some professions that he could go into without a degree.

Rob talks about a colleague telling him that he needed a change. He needed something new and fresh. Rob didn't recognize it but he was displaying discontent of some kind or his colleague would not have picked up on it.

We often can see things in others that we can't see in ourselves. Many times that feeling of being stuck just needs to be identified by someone else and then we're on our way. We all know someone that needs to be doing something different in some aspect of their life but they don't see it for themselves.

Sometimes it is fear that keeps us from looking at the aspects of our lives where we feel stuck. Whenever we make changes in our lives, fear is there to remind us that we are expanding beyond the life we have known.

Sometimes a little nudge from someone who cares about us is all it takes to make the first step. Walk with fear and you will expand your life into these new opportunities that your Crystalline Moments open up for you.

One of the things I was most impressed with in my conversation with Rob is his ability to follow his inner voice or guidance. When he recognized he needed help in planning his dream, he sought professionals to help him make a plan. They made him make a plan not just for his dream business but also for his life because all aspects of our lives are intertwined. When developing a dream, we need to take into consideration our health, relationships, career or creative expression and financial freedom because one affects the other. Most people spend more time and money on planning a vacation that they ever do planning for their lives.

The sooner we listen to our longings and discontent, the sooner and easier it will be to see the vision of what we were put on this earth to do. Then we need to write the vision down. We need to ask ourselves, what is the one thing I can do today that will get me one step closer to my dream?

Rob talks about how important it was for him to have a purpose that would help others. Actually any dream cannot come to fruition unless there is something in it that will help someone else.

By germinating and growing his idea, he formed and built his company, Down Payment Resource. He has created a national database of all the different down payment assistance programs that are available in different parts of the country. His company now helps people to have the ability to purchase the homes of their dreams.

How incredible it is that his Crystalline Moments in his life are now helping others have their own Crystalline Moments and living in the homes of their dreams.

To find out more about his company and the programs available for home down payment assistance, visit his website at: www.downpaymentresource.com.

7 ANDREW BEAM

"I reflected on my life. I was done, thinking of killing myself. I had just given up. This is it; I'm ready to go..."

Rob was just a young man when he started having Crystalline Moments that would lead him to the company of his dreams. His experience was different from Kenzie's moments in that Kenzie's Crystalline Moments are a gift that provides her with designs. Rob found his dream through a series of Crystalline Moments and being open to the inner voice guiding him each time. Now we have Andrew, a very successful chef who was living the life of his dreams until an incident happened.

In his early years, Andrew cooked for major celebrities and served as chef for Frank Sinatra at his home in Palm Springs, CA. Later, he held successful positions as head chef for several restaurants and a country club in the Portland, OR area.

This is a story of living the life of your dreams then because of an accident, your world comes crushing down into pain, suffering and addiction. Crystalline Moments helped Andrew during his amazing trials of recovery and ultimately saving his own life.

I've known Andrew Beam for many years. He is a very kind and wonderful man with an incredible passion for cooking. Being a chef is very difficult work and Andrew had been hurt a couple of different times in his career. We are going to pick Andrew's story up after he moved to Portland where I first met him.

****

Coni: I think a good place to start is when you ended up hurt on the job and tried to get on disability for your injury.

Andrew: I was here in Portland working since April 2001 at a country club in McMinnville, which is 45 minutes outside of the city. I wanted to move closer to home, so I took this job as a chef for a steakhouse in Portland. I took the job where for a year I took a pay cut with the understanding that there were going to be some insurance benefits.

Within a few months, I knew that was not going to happen. After about nine months, I started looking for other work. I found an ad for the Bubba Gump Shrimp Company that turned out to be working in their Hawaii location. I asked my wife, Rosemary, "Wouldn't it be great if I found a job there?!" She had always talked about living in Hawaii.

They called me right away and we negotiated a deal after I attended training at their offices in San Francisco. Originally, I was going to be the head chef for their restaurant in Maui but that changed to their Honolulu location.

Before we could leave, we needed to sell our house, most of our belongings—everything. Right before leaving the restaurant in Portland, I had a weird fall so my hip was bothering me. I headed to San Francisco for my training and five weeks in, I had another weird fall. It was bad. I had been working as an executive chef for 20 years and this was my big break, something I had always wanted.

I didn't let anyone know how badly I was hurt. But in the training program, we worked 12 to 14 hours a day, sometimes seven days a week. One day, they saw me struggling. At that point, I really couldn't lift my left leg to walk. I would just kind of drag and shuffle it behind me. They told me I would need to go back to Portland and fix this. So I went back for a few weeks and saw a bunch of doctors. It was never diagnosed properly. Most alluded it was just some kind of strain.

I convinced them that I could go back to work. I was never in any danger of losing the job in Hawaii initially, but eventually if I stayed out of training, I would lose the position in Hawaii and may be sent to some other state. I already had my plane ticket, I already had a place to stay. I was mentally already living and working in Hawaii.

They sent me to Long Beach, CA to finish up my training. About 10 days later in the middle of the day, I had a meltdown right there at work. I had 65 people I was in charge of looking to me for answers. I went into the office because I couldn't face anyone. I had a complete breakdown in front of the manager. I was just completely overwhelmed and physically incapable of doing my job. A few days later, on October 29, 2007, that was it for me.

In my mind, I had worked so hard for so many years and nailed this, but now I had let everyone down. My wife and I had already gotten rid of all of our possessions. I felt my whole world fall apart.

In two years, in October 2009, my wage benefits stopped. My pending case was not settled and now we couldn't pay our mortgage.

In December, the doctor in San Francisco who was in charge of the case said in a report that the injury was not caused in San Francisco but in Portland while still working at the steakhouse. That pretty much ended my case in California.

I discovered from the Oregon doctor that the case had never been closed there, so I found an attorney. She managed to reopen the case because the final doctor who saw me in Portland said they did not find me perfectly stationary, but that they will release me to return to work. That was the key to reopening the case.

We had to start all over with everything again. In the meantime, there's no money. We lost our home, they took our cars, we went through bankruptcy. This was December 2011. My wife went to Australia for her work, and I knew when she came back we weren't going to be together. I spent that Christmas moving to a friend's basement after I got everything packed up in the house.

The following October, I got a call from Rosemary that her mother was dying. She'd had cancer for two years but had chemo and her doctor said she was cleared of cancer. But about four months later, they found the cancer had come back.

This cancer was in her cells. That was it. She was woman I was very close to...someone I'd known for 30 years who didn't care what had happened between me and Rosemary. She told me on her deathbed that I was the son she never had. I went to her house in Red Bluff, CA to see her for myself and to support the family. My plan was to just go for a few days. Things were much worse than I had imagined. Rosemary and I agreed that we would alternate every two weeks with her sister in coming to take care of her mom.

When our turn was up, we went back to Portland but then I got the call she was dying. She died before Rosemary or I got back to her home.

We planned everything. We had this big celebration of life. Emotionally, I'm a wreck at this point. It was during this time that Rosemary told me she was seeing someone, but I found out she was actually living with this person. I started asking questions and she finally admitted it. It was someone I knew. I was crushed. The way we had been talking, I had thought there was a chance for us up until then.

I told everyone that I was doing fine. I was just focusing on helping get things done on Mom's house. Since I had lost a lot of weight through bariatric surgery from my disability program, I had been feeling pretty good. I started walking every day for several reasons. There were times I needed to get out of the house, plus I needed to get away from my mental state as much as possible. I would walk to this place that I had lived for a period of time. It was a trailer park right on the Sacramento River where I had lived with a girlfriend many years previous. I reflected on my life. I was done, thinking of killing myself. I had just given up. This is it; I'm ready to go.

There's a bridge right there over the Sacramento River. This is the perfect time and place, I thought. The river was extremely low and very rocky. I would just walk up and jump. The only thing that was holding me back was the fear that I would jump, live and be paralyzed.

I had my headphones on listening to music and crying. I walked up to the bridge but then I heard this eagle cry. I looked to see where this eagle was. He was a couple hundred yards away but coming in my direction. I'm watching it and realize that it's coming straight at me.

I'm now on the bank about 15 feet above the river. All of a sudden, this bird was right above me. When it got right there, it put its huge wings back and stayed there hovering and did this big giant loop above me. Then it just took off.

That was a huge Crystalline Moment for me! It was in those few moments that I decided I wanted to live. I just wasn't sure how. What I didn't know was that things were about to get even worse for me.

I was drinking quite a bit and there was something else going on. I had been on pain pills for 20 years due to various other job injuries during my career. It was always within the boundaries of the doctor's prescription, but I had wanted to wean myself off of them before the hip surgery that I needed soon.

I started weaning myself off and after I got to the end of my medication, I began having withdrawal symptoms. I drank more to compensate for the symptoms and all the mental stuff I was going through.

By the time I got back to Portland after getting Mom's house in order, I was drinking very heavily. I had to go back on pain pills. I started drinking even more. I was still functioning for a while, only drinking at bars in the evening. I never drank when I was alone.

In February, I went out one night to a bar and don't remember finishing the first drink. According to the information we have now, I was drugged with something called GHB. It's the date rape drug that makes people have blackout experiences.

Police reports said I got in my car and crashed into my neighbor's brand new Dodge Caravan. I refused the drunk driving test so they took me downtown.

After that incident, things went downhill. I started drinking around the clock, really isolating myself. I didn't know whether it was day or night. I had a panic attack and knew if I didn't do something about this today—immediately—I was going to die. I'd never had panic attacks before...always cool, calm and collected, so I knew this was real.

I needed to do something anyway because of the court case. I contacted my court liaison who told me to go to this place called Hooper Detox. I was told I had to be there between 6:45-7:45 AM. That was not a problem because I was getting up around 4:30 AM anyway. I would wake up needing a drink so I wouldn't shake so bad in order for me to get dressed.

This was a Friday. My friend agreed to drive me. We got there early, so I fixed a 32 oz. cocktail before we left and drank that on the way. We got there right at 6:55 AM and I went in. I had to fill out a one-page intake form. They closed and locked the doors at 7:45 AM so you had to be inside by then. From that time until they fill available beds, you have to sit there and wait.

On that day, we counted 43 people and they only took two. We were told we could go but not to leave until we saw the triage nurse. Now I had to wait until Monday because they didn't take people over the weekend. If you didn't come back and be there on Monday, your name goes back to the bottom of the list.

I freaked out, expecting to get in. It's now 9 AM and the liquor stores didn't open for a couple of hours. What was I going to do? I begged the nurse to let me stay. "No, you can't," she said, "but please, do NOT stop drinking." She said three things can kill you from Detox - heroine, methadone and alcohol. I assured her that not drinking wasn't even possible.

It was a horrible weekend. I had to go buy more booze three or four times. On Monday morning, there were 48 people there. I didn't get in. I went back on Tuesday and didn't get in. I'm wondering, how long is it going to take?

Some suggested that I go to a hospital, but hospitals don't care about alcoholics. You really need to be in a Detox facility. Finally on Wednesday, they took me and I spent 10 days there.

It was a fantastic program, great doctors and after a week, the nurses told me I was physically cleared to go, but I said no. I was not ready, so they let me stay. A few days later, my head felt clear and I told them I'm ready to leave.

I felt like a man fresh out of prison, but I still had a lot of things to work through. Bad things still ran around my head, however, I was pretty much re-born again.

I can't remember the accident thing, but I remember everything else. I went to AA meetings every day. I went through my state board program. The following February, I got my driver's license back and I went back to court. All my charges were dismissed.

Coni: So what is it like now for you?

Andrew: I still had to come to terms that my marriage was over. We are amicable and have worked through all the issues. I have a girlfriend that I really care about and it's nice to be back in a relationship. I go to AA meetings every Saturday morning. I find I can be helpful to others.

Coni: When you are able to see how you can be of service to others, it also helps you see how you can be of service to yourself. You are able to get back in tune with your inner self and to see what the next step is going to be. You are more open to accepting and receiving those opportunities that Crystalline Moments provide.

Andrew: Yes, of all the things that have happened to me since I got hurt in 2007, I thought they were the end of the world, they were destroying me. Instead, they were a blessing in disguise.

My separation and getting a divorce were a blessing. My DUI was a blessing and thank God no one got hurt. I don't know if I could live with the thought that I had hurt someone. Each of these moments has brought such clarity and opportunity to my life.

Coni: That is a very important point. When we have something happen that we feel is the end of the world, it is really the Universe changing our course and making us wake up to the opportunities that lie ahead. After an incident in my 20's that sent my world upside down, I realized that everything happens for a positive reason. We just don't really know what it is at the time. Now when anything happens that appears to be the worst thing ever, I tell myself that there is a positive reason for this.

Andrew: That is exactly right. That is how I feel about everything I have been through. I'm sure there will be other ups and downs but I now know to look for the opportunity and I know there is some lesson I need to learn or something great is going to come out of it.

****

Some of us ignore our inner voice; we don't pay attention to pebbles, stones, rocks or boulders. We have to hit rock bottom before we start listening.

Andrew's story is not a singular story. I just watched a special on television about the astronomical number of people that are addicted to pain pills and turn to heroine as a cheap alternative. His story can give hope to those that are looking for a way out of addiction.

The eagle that appeared and stopped him from suicide was a momentous Crystalline Moment! One of the things he said was that he had no idea how he was going to move forward but he knew he would be okay.

No matter whether a moment is something positive or something as serious as saving someone's life, you will probably not know immediately what the future holds. Take notice when you have thoughts and then move a singular step in the direction of the life of your dreams. When you do that, another step will appear.

Andrew came to the point that he knew he was going to die from alcohol if he did not get into Detox. That realization, that Crystalline Moment, provided the opportunity for him to start on the path of recovery and living the life of his dreams.

8 KEVIN JORGESON

"That moment when you decide to do it rather than thinking about doing it is a moment of clarity..."

Andrew's story is a journey from the deepest of despair to the joys of having the life of his dreams. Henry David Thoreau in his famous quote regarding the Walden Pond experiment says, "I have learned this, at least, by my experiment. That if one advances confidently in the direction of their dream, endeavoring to live the life they are imagining, one passes an invisible boundary..."

When he says *"endeavoring,"* he means that it won't be a perfect journey but we will reach the top of the mountain's *"invisible boundary"*. When that happens, people and opportunities will start just showing up that will help us move toward our dream.

As you climb a mountain, you will sometimes move up and other times move sideways as you maneuver around rocks and boulders. Then when you reach the top, you can finally see what is on the other side. Those Crystalline Moments are the rocks and the boulders that you maneuver around to reach the top. Once at the top, you will see the life you would love.

This next conversation I love because it is literally about climbing rocks. I met Kevin and his girlfriend, Jacqui, when they first came to visit my home as Airbnb guests. I have now adopted them.

Kevin is an internationally-known professional rock climber. I use a talk he gave at the Google corporate offices as part of my workshop entitled, *Turning Your Dreams into Destiny*. I put Kevin's story into this book because our lives, our Crystalline Moments, are a lot like rock climbing.

Kevin as a small child climbed on and up everything. It was a natural progression for him to start rock climbing. His parents created a good balance for him as his father always let him take risks, but his mother was always pulling her hair out worrying about him.

He has been sponsored for rock climbing since he was 16, and as of this writing, he is 29 years old. He started climbing near his home in Santa Rosa, California. One of the things he told me, which took me by surprise, was that there are people in their 90's that are still rock climbing.

After reading this intimate conversation, you will want to go out and climb your own Dawn Wall!

****

Coni: When you are climbing rocks, what is it about? When you get to the top of a rock, what is the feeling? Is it euphoria...success...I did it?

Kevin: It's fun, first of all and I love doing it. It kind of depends on what the struggle to reach the top was like. There is a direct correlation to how much of a fight you had to do to get to the top.

Coni: Tell us about your current project of creating a new rock climbing route up the face, called the Dawn Wall, of El Capitan in Yosemite. When do you hope to finish with the route?

Kevin: It has been six years at this time and several hundred days exclusively on the Dawn Wall. We are taking it like an assault approach. We're coming in at the top and we work sections; we come in from the bottom and work. We are all over the face of this rock. What is interesting is that in the beginning, I wasn't sure it would be possible to create this route at all. My partner completely believed it was possible so I had to believe in his belief until I finally believed it could be done.

The goal is to be able to start at the bottom and go up through the pitches without having to come back down or falling. If you fall, you go back to the start of that pitch. Pitches are about every 200 feet and there are about 35 pitches on this rock. Every season is different but we focus on different pitches until we get them right. We hope to finish this year.

When we are finished, the route could take about two weeks to ascend from bottom to top. We fix lines on the route in order to be able to reach all of the areas we need to work on. Then when we climb, one person starts up connected to the rope. Then we leapfrog our way up.

Coni: I love the pictures of you camping out on the side of the wall, especially the ones of you having coffee. Sitting on the side of this rock and drinking from your French press is quite a dichotomy. It must be an outrageous feeling.

Kevin: It is awesome, a perspective a lot of people don't get to have. It's great though to be up there. Yeah, I take my French press everywhere.

Coni: I know you have climbed all over the world. What are some of the moments you would describe as Crystalline Moments?

Kevin: That moment when you decide to do it rather than thinking about doing it is a moment of clarity. I'm very calculating about my climbing. You have to be very intentional when you are doing something this dangerous. You need a certain amount of fear. That is very healthy.

Coni: What kind of training do you do to prepare for a climb?

Kevin: I do cross training. As it gets closer, I do more conditioning, more cardio. Just so you can get into the place where you crux pitch, you have to either go to the top and rappel down, or you have to start at the bottom ascending the fix line. Either way, it is a brutal cardio workout.

Coni: How do you stay up there? I saw a picture that looked like you were standing there with just your fingers hanging onto the wall.

Kevin: It's like a dance. Your hands are like your feet and your feet are like your hands. All four limbs are working together. You put chalk on your fingers to help you grip. The shoes you wear are very, very tight climbing shoes. They have sticky rubber on the bottom.

Coni: Certainly not for the faint of heart! I am completely inspired by what you do even though I have no intention of rock climbing. I see that rock climbing is a metaphor for identifying our Crystalline Moments and living the life of our dreams. We could all use sticky rubber-soled shoes as we are maneuvering our own boulders in life. Just so we could hang on!

Kevin: I love to think that someone is inspired by what I do. It is a good by-product.

Coni: Do you have a mentor?

Kevin: I have used a coach while climbing who was very inspirational and helpful. The climbing community is a global community. You can find rock climbers anywhere in the world. We are all on common ground and there is inspiration throughout the community.

Coni: If someone wants to start rock climbing, where do they start?

Kevin: Go to the gym and find a good instructor and take lessons. Also, find a good mentor or coach.

Coni: What part of the overall experience do you find most gratifying? Is it the feat itself or the accomplishment when you are done?

Kevin: It is the process; it never ends. You start with everything you do to plan a climb then move to everything involved to complete the climb. Then you move on to the next climb.

You choose your own path of resistance. If you want to challenge yourself, you can, or if you want to cruise along, you can do that too.

****

There is so much about rock climbing that is a metaphor for all of us in using our Crystalline Moments and creating opportunity from them to live the life of our dreams. When Kevin decides his next climb, or as he calls it, project, that is his Crystalline Moment.

Let's dissect how we can use rock climbing to become clear on how to take advantage of the opportunities our own Crystalline Moments offer us.

First, we define what the opportunities are that we are given. For Kevin, that is deciding on the next climb. Is it going to be difficult or does he want to cruise?

Second, we make the decision that we are going to move forward with the opportunity that is given to us. The first thing Kevin talks about is the plan. Our plan is to put one foot in front of another and our dream will unfold as we move forward. In designing the route up the Dawn Wall, Kevin and his partner need to adjust the route as they move forward.

Kevin talks about what the feeling is like when he reaches the top. He says it depends on how much of a struggle it was to reach it. That determines his sensation when he reaches the top.

We all have something we are struggling with to climb our mountain and live the life of our dreams. It could be fear, it could be we are not coming from gratitude, or we are not in alignment with our dream.

With fear, we embrace and move with it to reach our dreams. He talks about fear and how important it is to have healthy fear when climbing. Fear is our companion on the journey; it is actually the energy of the border of the reality that we know.

Kevin talks about healthy fear, and for us, it is not in the absence of fear but in the presence of fear and how we manage it. If someone is rock climbing and does it without fear, they will not have the respect needed for the rock to achieve the goal of making it to the top. We use our fear as a stepping stone to move forward just like we would if we were climbing.

The project of creating a new rock climbing route up the Dawn Wall of El Capitan has taken many years to complete. All along the way, our Crystalline Moments are like each pitch on the rock. They get us that much closer to the top of our mountain.

Our dreams may take several years for us to achieve. As long as we are looking at it from the point of living our dream, those pitches will close the gap.

Fix lines are used at different pitches so that climbers can move around the rock. We have fix lines as well. They are goals that we achieve when we take those steps that get us that much closer to living our dreams.

If we reach a goal and it is not quite what is going to move us forward, we go back to the previous spot and redefine our 'fix line' for that pitch. Kevin has 35 pitches on El Capitan. We have four areas of our lives that must be in alignment - health, relationships, creative expression or career, and financial freedom. We crux pitch between these areas and sometimes we fall and have to go back to the previous pitch.

He mentions being able to have an amazing perspective camping on the side of the rock that many people are not able to experience. We all have our own amazing life perspective that we can look at with gratitude and drink from our own French coffee press.

Climbing is calculated and intentional. When we grasp the opportunity of our Crystalline Moments, we also must be intentional and calculate what we need to do to move forward.

Kevin further talks about doing cross training so he can be prepared to rappel or ascend a fix line. We too must train to be able to rappel down, or ascend up our own fix lines. We need to be able to navigate and adjust the direction we are heading based on where the opportunities are taking us. Our dream is organic and will grow and expand as we grow and expand.

With feet and hands in unison, Kevin likens climbing to a dance. That is why we cannot focus on just one of the four areas of our lives and ignore the others. Our life is a dance. If our four areas are not in unison with our dream, then we will fall. As we rappel or ascend between the different areas of our lives, we may need to adjust the fix line that connects each area to keep them all in alignment. When we align our path, we create an expansion of all areas of our life. We create the perfect dance!

To grow stronger and be able to identify our Crystalline Moments and make the decision to seize the opportunity those moments bring, we need to continue to nurture our brains and take advantage of all of the resources out there that can help us.

Cross training with a great mentor or coach will help us to identify which muscles need more work, just like a trainer helps someone know which training is going to be beneficial for their body and physical goals.

Kevin states that when he finishes with one project, he goes on to the next. As we move toward our dreams, our dreams grow larger and our life expands. We all can choose to design our lives or cruise by living life by default.

He is also now helping others learn to climb by investing in rock climbing gyms around the country and by speaking about the sport. When you hear him talk, you can't help but be inspired to climb whatever El Capitan you are supposed to climb in your life.

If you would like to learn more about Kevin Jorgeson, please visit his website at: www.kevinjorgeson.com.

He is truly an inspiration to us all. Let your next Crystalline Moment take you to the top of your El Capitan!

9 KATHIE NELSON

"I will never be in this position again!"

Kevin's journey as an internationally-known rock climber has given him the gift of understanding how to find opportunity in his moments to create an amazing life he loves. He is doing exactly what he was put on this earth to do. His dream expands by every new rock he climbs.

Just like the way that Kevin takes on rock climbing, Kathie has taken on her own El Capitan life and had to create her own route.

Kathie's life started out by attending private school. Her father was in the military and when he retired, he had gone back to school to become a teacher. He'd come from a very traditional family believing that boys learned certain things and girls learned something different.

When she graduated from high school, like many girls at that time, the only thing she knew was that she wanted to be a wife and mom. In the 1950's, the primary role of girls and women were that of housewives and mothers. Few went on to have careers, although some would find jobs mainly to support their families.

Kathie's story is about what happened to so many young women during that time. She married at 20, had her first child at 21 and was divorced by 22 years old.

Her story is also one of how to move forward through Crystalline Moments and to journey through the opportunities they offer. Kathie's life of helping others shows us no matter what your circumstances are, if we use our life experiences as the stepping stones to the life of our dreams, then we can all achieve our greatness.

Kathie Nelson grew up the middle child of a family of five children. She describes herself today as a great mom, a spitfire, military brat, entrepreneur, visionary and a believer both literally and figuratively in other people.

In high school, she graduated in three years but like so many girls at that time, really didn't know what she wanted to do. So what did she do? She went to work at a deli.

My conversation with Kathie shows how she found a mentoring opportunity in every part of her life. Nothing that happens in our lives is by accident.

She is now a successful speaker, author, coach and consultant. Kathie travels all over the world speaking.

****

Coni: What was your first career?

Kathie: I worked at a deli. That job taught me a lot. I was taught the etiquette of providing service. I did some cooking and since it was a fast order place, I also learned the cash register. When I think about it, I realize how much that job taught me real life skills.

From there, I got a job at a bank in the Northwest. I was the drive-thru teller and worked there for a year. I learned bookkeeping at that job—another great experience that I have used my entire life.

After that, I got a job at a credit union. It was smaller than the bank and I learned more about banking. I was still very young, only 20. It was then that I met my first husband and we got engaged. Then I went to work for a radio station and ran the air traffic.

There I started working with computers, when they still had floppy drives. I worked with and supported the sales reps. So now I have picked up some computer skills and started learning about sales and reps.

When I was 21 years old, I married and had my first child. I stopped working and became a stay-at-home mom. That was my dream from when I graduated high school. I stayed home with my son for about 10 months.

Unbeknownst to me because I was so young, not working and having a child put a strain on the relationship. Things became very stressful and my husband decided he didn't want to be married anymore.

That's when I got one of my first real Crystalline Moments. Here I was. I had a husband that didn't want to be married, I had a child, no money, no job, nothing of my own. I was fiercely committed to protecting my child and my moment was, "I will never be in this position again!"

When this type of moment happens, we go down to our basic survival instincts. I became completely clear about the need to take control of my life.

Coni: There are so many women, including myself, that find themselves in this position and make that oath. It changes your life forever. In a way, it cleanses you.

Kathie: We are hard-wired to be in community. We are not designed to go it alone. At times when we are in relationships, we allow our souls to be fractured. The clarity reminds us that we are the creators of our own lives. I was divorced at 22 and the following year, I was in a severe auto accident. The year after that, I remarried and had my second child at 25.

Coni: How did the car accident affect your life?

Kathie: I found myself in a very similar place as when my first husband wanted to leave so he could be happy. I had to stay home because of my injuries. The car accident was very similar in that I didn't know how I was going to take care of myself. They told me I would never walk again and that I would be handicapped for the rest of my life.

Once again, I had a life-changing Crystalline Moment where I became crystal clear about how I would work around my inability to walk. I made an oath and refused to accept the fact that doctors told me I would never walk again.

Coni: The perseverance of going through that process must have made a huge effect on the rest of your life.

Kathie: You create this belief system you work from that is there from previous life experiences. I was a middle child so I had to prove myself. It's easy to get lost in a bunch of kids. Next I got a divorce, so now I am going to prove that I can make it on my own.

When I was in the car accident, I felt at a loss. I didn't have the ability to walk. I was in incredible pain and had horrific scars because a guard rail had wrapped around my leg. Being a woman, I wanted to wear dresses and nice shoes so in addition to everything else, I felt even more at a deficit. So now I have a filter that says, "I have to prove that I am more than because I am less than."

Coni: How long was it before you were able to take the first steps?

Kathie: My accident was in March 1984 and I was walking by the end of the year with crutches and leg braces. Because I was determined to get back to full functionality, I went back to work part-time in January 1985. I had to prove that I could do everything I had done before.

It wasn't too difficult because I worked for a telecom company and I was handling customer service and the phones. It meant that I could get out, be with people and function in the workplace. I really should have taken more time at home because the job was in Eugene, Oregon and I was living in Southern Oregon with my parents...an hour's drive away.

I finally was able to move to Eugene to be close to my work. My son and I moved into a small apartment. I'm still on crutches and leg braces but living on my own. It was a very crazy time when I think back about it.

Coni: How long was it before you went to work with Norman Apparel?

Kathie: I first became acquainted with Norman Apparel (a clothes shopping service) in 1993. That was after I had started my own telecom company in Portland and it failed. Again, there was the whole proving thing...filter, that I can do anything. My dad told me I was smart and I could figure out anything.

So now I had two filters working: one that was "I could do anything" and one that was "I had to prove myself." I took a risk in starting the business and it failed.

I came through the back door to Norman Apparel. I loved their product and wore their product. I hated shopping because of all of the challenges that come with that. As I was introduced to them and began to play with their program, I saw the challenges.

I clicked with the entrepreneurial component of direct sales, even though I said I was never going to sell. I liked it because there was no one telling me that I had to do anything. I loved helping other people. There were no quotas and I could do whatever I wanted...cash is addictive. It is always great when people pay you for something you love to do.

I played with it for six to nine months working part-time. Then I went to a conference in Chicago and saw what other women were doing. I saw women being entrepreneurs and building an organization. I knew I could do that. I can do anything!

No matter what anyone says about direct sales or network marketing, it is rich with personal development opportunities. If you can get your mind around the fact that it is a business rather than a money-making scheme—there are exceptions—it is a solid business model. It allows you to serve a client base and be compensated for your services by expanding and building your own sales team. You have to come at it from that perspective, which is not the way some companies train.

Coni: How many sales associates did you have?

Kathie: At one time I had 70 people. I was a top recruiter and once I was recognized for sales, I never missed an incentive. Being in that environment, there was a tremendous amount of self-discovery.

That environment provided me with another Crystalline Moment in that it offered validation in two ways; first the need to prove myself. The second was the filter, "I have to overachieve so people will notice me so I don't get lost in the crowd." It was not about winning or the prize.

After I lost the telecom company, I had gone to work for a cardiac monitoring and surgical laser company. The boss I had was brilliant but he was also diabolical at times. He had a way of inspiring me but it was with a hook. The hook was, "I have to work harder, then even harder." I was working 80 hours a week when I found the Weekender opportunity, another direct sales (clothing service) company. I started Weekenders part-time while I was at that job.

Coni: That is a Crystalline Moment many people have had. When you realize you deserve better than the way you are being treated. You're excelling and excelling because you think the validation and the pay will be there, but you are just being taken advantage of.

Kathie: Yes, if you were raised by anyone that went through the Depression, you were raised with the message if you just work hard enough, people will recognize it and you will be compensated for it. In a small business, you can only rise to a certain level and there's only so much money in the budget for pay. Your boss allocates how much there is for payroll.

If they have any residual thoughts that women only deserve to have a certain amount, or a certain role, no matter what you do, you are not going to get the validation. For me, it was like that perfect storm between my own personal beliefs and the guy I worked with.

I worked harder, was given more responsibility and learned a lot. In that respect, it was great. I learned how to run an international company, run inventory, run position training and how to travel internationally by myself.

But my family was suffering. I couldn't get away and I was killing myself. So that Crystalline Moment comes when you ask yourself, at what point did I think I deserved to be treated like this and allow this job to define me. I started with Weekender full-time and worked for them for 12 years, resigning in 2002.

Coni: So is that when you started your company, Connectworks?

Kathie: It is. One of my Crystalline Moments was on 9/11. I was on my way to a networking meeting, but was watching the planes and didn't believe it was happening. I went to my breakfast appointment with this gal from a networking franchise that I was considering buying.

I am sitting there talking to her, but I keep having the plane images run through my mind. I told the gal that I really didn't feel at peace about this and would go home and think about it.

When I got home, I turned on the TV and saw what was happening. I started thinking about all the people I had met through Weekender from all over the U.S. I could know these people; we could have crossed paths. I asked myself, what am I doing?

For me, it was never about the clothes. It was always about the people. Being able to equip individuals so they could show up and excel. I was able to bring this strategic networking philosophy to the wardrobing concept. I never worried about sales...I could always make the sales.

That moment is when I realized that this vehicle, Weekenders, was only going to get me so far. I realized that it would limit my ability to speak at the core of strategic networking and not allow me to build something that could empower people. I had never stayed at a job longer than a year and a half. I would get bored. After 12 years, I had proven what I could do and had made a mark. I had found myself.

Coni: Did you feel at that point that you were living the life you loved?

Kathie: I was getting close. That was part of the reason I had stayed for 12 years. I was able to get more and more aligned and more congruent.

The entrepreneurial aspect when you start your own business, or you join a business where you are key to business development is that you don't read the small print that says, you signed up for the most intensive personal development training school of your life.

I kept looking at the things that were limiting me and what I could change, whether it was in my mind or my process for that continuous improvement. As I moved through the process of running my own business, I had allowed all of my stories to define me after they had first derailed me. We all allow first our stories to derail us, then we allow them to define us.

Then ultimately, they will refine us when we shed the story and we become who we are meant to be. They only define us if we let them.

When I look back at the accident, the divorce and the choices I made that put hardship on me because of my need to prove myself, I realized that even though things happened to me, I created the things that happened and chose how to respond.

So what is it that I have learned to be true about me? What is true about the world and what is true about the passion and purpose that is in our DNA? The creator of the Universe embedded it into our DNA which is why we can't get rid of our purpose. That is why we long to be aligned with our dreams.

So those 10-12 years of intensive sales training and building a company had caused me to look at my purpose and passion. I noticed where I was incongruent in myself. I'm saying this but I'm doing that. I'm out of alignment. It creates a physical or visceral response in us that makes us feel disconnected and discontent.

Coni: So now that you have had your own successful networking and speaking business, what do you think are the things you have learned and know most about yourself?

Kathie: We grow up with a self-image based on our childhood environment. Our personality preferences, our styles, our psychological drivers are in us and then they are shaped by the environment we grow up in.

Then we have these soul barbs that want to keep us from becoming what we want to be. As we travel through life, we get these layers of things added to our DNA. At every point along the way, the creator of the Universe is after us to restore us to our original state. Some people call it the Universe. I prefer to call it the creator of the Universe. When our inner voice says, I am not happy with this, the contradiction of where I am and where I want to be causes us to question the Universe and where we are going.

A Crystalline Moment...I'm 38 and I am close to turning 40 and I say to myself, "God, I can't believe you want to create us to be miserable. Having these highs and these lows and never quite getting it. So God, if you are so brilliant, so amazing and so who you say you are...why this?"

It came down to what you believe about yourself is not true. I had spent my time living outside of my body watching my life until this revelation. My family was always so concerned about my future…all parents want you to be this or don't be that. Think about it as parents; we have all done it.

When the "being that" is a natural state, you're saying it's not okay to be yourself. So when I grew up and would behave in a natural way that didn't fit into the beliefs that I had been taught, it was not a good thing. It was "be this way" or "that way" because of my programming. In other words, I grew up saying that it was not okay to be me.

At 38, I said I'm not going to live this way anymore. I needed to find out what was true. I have a fundamental belief that I was created by the creator of the Universe for a purpose. I needed to find out about everything. I went to the scriptures and searched for everything that was true about me.

I started a little index of note cards and every time something would trigger a thought like, "There I go again…I'm always going to screw up…I have to prove this…" – all those filters or messages through which I saw the world, I would stop it. I would actually put my fingers on the middle of my forehead and stop it.

I learned years later through neuroplasticity that our brains can be completely rewired and the frontal lobe is where thought gets stopped. I would put my fingers on my forehead and stop the thought, then I would go to my cards and say what is true. What is true is, God says, "I knew you when you were in your mother's womb. I wrote your name on my hand. Before the foundations of the world knew you, I knew you."

This started changing the way I thought about myself. Over time, I started to get into my own body. Then I would notice and feel differently when I was out of alignment. We all long to be who we are and be known by others for who we are. We are spiritual beings having a human experience.

Coni: Over the years that I have been following you, I found you to be a great inspiration through your speaking and your writing.

Kathie: I love that I found I could write, even though my college professor said I would pass his writing class but I'd never become a writer. Haven't we all heard that? We've all been told we're not good enough to do something. As I began to write about the things I have learned, I asked myself the question, how do I get unstuck? When you feel compelled to do something, listen to that voice and do it. When you do, you are honoring yourself and honoring other people.

****

In Kathie's story, she talks a lot about filters. We all have our family environments that work to shape our lives. If we don't notice what we are thinking about, we will not recognize thought processes that may be interfering with the reason we have been put on this earth.

It is important for us to analyze and understand when we are living our lives as our authentic self and when we need to get back into alignment. When we question where we are going, we should write down what our purpose is and what our vision for our lives is.

In order to live the life of our dreams, we must have a blueprint to follow. If we don't, we will allow our conditions and circumstances to dictate what direction we want to go in. It doesn't matter whether we call that energy source God, the

Creator of the Universe, Mindset, Allah or any other term. We all have the ability to choose to put out the energy that will create what our life purpose and visions are.

Kathie's Crystalline Moments all came down to her choosing to live her life with the purpose and vision of why she was put on this earth. She is now living the life of her dreams. Whether it is divorce, loss or health issues, we can all choose to live a life in alignment with our purpose.

Kathie has written several books. One is called *How do Busy People get Unstuck*, and she co-wrote another with her mom, *I Want What She's Got*. She contributed to another bestseller with the Direct Sales Association called *101 Insider Secrets*. She is working on another book right now that is soon to be released.

Kathie's website is www.kathienelson.com. Her program, Get Monetized Now, is a learning & growth community designed to serve leaders in tenacious pursuit of the flow that occurs when passion, purpose and profit intersect.

10 JULIE RENEE DOERING

*"I was promised the Garden of Eden, but was
- living a hell, a hell on earth. And it was
because I hadn't asked for more..."*

Kathie Nelson's journey from an insecure wife and mother to international writer and speaker is a path that few of us as women have taken. We often choose a life that we have been told to take either from our parents, our spouses or how we perceive the world wants us to live.

It is only through design that we change who and what we want to be. We all have 525,600 minutes in a year! We can design how those minutes are going to be used or we can default to our conditions and circumstances to decide for us.

The next intimate conversation is one that will take the idea of designing our lives to a whole new level. Just like Kathie, Julie Renee was a young mother and had major health issues as a young woman. Hers is definitely a story of being in the wrong place at the wrong time, and from that journey, recognizing her gifts and abilities on a plane that most of us will probably never reach, even though we all have the capacity to do so.

As a young girl, Julie Renee was traveling on vacation with her parents across the Nevada desert when the government was testing atomic bombs. While there, she was exposed to radioactive material that created a life of illness and near-death experiences.

I met Julie Renee at a conference on how to present on stage (preparing myself for events once this book was published). She was one of the presenters and when I heard her story, it blew me away. I had to meet her. I also knew I had to include her in this book.

In many ways, Julie Renee's story is very similar in the beginning to Kathie's with one very notable exception: her exposure to radioactive material from the Nevada Atomic Test Site. She is very fortunate to be a survivor and go on to be able to offer help to people suffering in all aspects of life. She received enough toxic exposure to turn her youthful health into a fight for her life at age 24.

This is how she describes that time in her book, *100% You Formula*. "In short order, I had seventeen surgeries, multiple cancers, and five Near-Death experiences in which I died twice. I spent a year in a wheelchair and was told I would never walk without pain and that I would need to rely on canes."

****

Coni: First, I must ask. Do you recall any Crystalline Moments when you were actually exposed to the radioactive material?

Julie Renee: I wouldn't say there were any moments at the time of the exposure, but there were many moments in my 20's when I was facing terminal cancer. One of them was when I was having trouble staying awake.

I went to the doctor and told him I just could not keep my eyes open. I was pregnant and what they discovered was terminal cancer. I was four months pregnant, a born-again Christian and they mentioned the word abortion.

They knew they wouldn't get anywhere with me...they just mentioned it and went on. Right then, I made a decision to provide life to my child. I pleaded with God to please save my baby.

What that plead produced was a baby that was born on his exact due date and he was 8 pounds. This was from a cancer-ridden mother that was 5'6" and only 104 pounds. That beautiful baby boy was an absolute miracle of life.

Once he was born, I was in the fight for my life. When he was about 8 months old, I collapsed in my living room. That was one of the times when life left my body. At that point, I was only 96 pounds. They told me that they expected me to die within two weeks.

When I was reaching the end of the two-week period and they were expecting me to pass, I collapsed again. This time I was alone and no one was with me. Again, I was a spirit looking down at my body.

My thought was, "Oh no, it's over." And then, "Oh no, it's not over." I saw my life fly by. All the scenes of my life fell before my eyes. I pushed myself back into my body and forced my spirit back in.

I forced myself to start eating; I hadn't eaten in two weeks. I'd had multiple surgeries on my neck which had given me a terrible unbearable pain to eat so I just stopped trying.

At that point, I plumped up. I decided that now I know I am supposed to be here for a reason. I know there is something special for me to do. I'm not supposed to die yet.

I turned it all around in six months. I had gained 50 pounds to the surprise of everyone. I was still very sick but the weight issues were gone. I went on to have more surgeries but the decision was that I was here to stay and I was here for a reason, no matter what happened.

Then there was a Crystalline Moment eight years ago in my garden. It came over a period of a week when I was in so much pain. By then I'd had 17 surgeries; I'd spent two years of my life in hospital beds; I had been in a wheelchair for a year. There was a 'come to Jesus moment' where I said I can't do this anymore.

I had worked on my will over the previous couple months, so I finished it. I called my oldest daughter and said, "Honey, I want you to pull the plug if anything bad happens and I will go." She said, "Mom, I don't want your money. I want you to stay!" But I said, 'You have to promise me if one more thing happens…because I don't want to do this anymore."

She agreed to do it. But then in my mind, I thought that maybe I was going about this the wrong way. I was thinking about it wrong. So over the course of the next few days, it dawned on me that I had begged, pleaded that I would survive, that I wanted to see my children grow up. But I had forgotten to put in the formula that I wanted a 100% healthy life. So what I did...I just survived!

Coni: Yes, the Universe gives us what we ask for!

Julie Renee: In that dawn, that wake-up Crystalline Moment, which lasted over the course of a week, I realized that I was promised the Garden of Eden, but was living a hell, a hell on earth. And it was because I hadn't asked for more. So I went to my garden and prayed.

I was convinced that I was willing to die, or be totally healed. One or the other! I was going to stay in that garden to pray and meditate until I was enlightened. I wanted to be like Buddha. He was told that he couldn't be enlightened because he was too wealthy. He was told that no son of a rich king will ever be enlightened. He stayed there for 40 days and became enlightened. Unlike Buddha, for me, it was instantaneous. In the first day, I watched myself start lining up in my perfected state.

In the last eight years I have developed a way to access the human blueprint with the quantum field and actually grow back glands and organs that have been surgically removed.

My life is incredible and when people hear my story, they can't believe it. They think I am 20 or 30 years younger than I actually am. There's no evidence, no outside evidence, that I was ever sick.

Coni: Absolutely amazing! Was it after your garden experience that you realized you had this special gift?

Julie Renee: I would say I always knew that I had a gift of healing. The wake-up call was the understanding about how much we can control and how good the gift can be. We make a choice of how we are going to live.

It seems unfathomable. I was going to all of these doctor's appointments, seeing all of these alternative people, and I was working on myself, taking supplements and exercising. I was doing everything I needed to do, but I hadn't changed the program patterns and mindset to be 100% healthy.

I think there's one thing we miss and that is if you don't believe that it is possible, then it is not going to be possible. If you believe you can be 100% healthy, then you are going to move towards a much higher ground than a person who is just surviving.

I'm talking about 100%. So many people want the 80-20 rule so they don't live full out. You must live in the realm of possibility that you can be 100%. That doesn't mean that you're perfect. It means that is the realm you live in.

Coni: I remember when you said that you realized you had this gift and how you became ill and went off by yourself. Was that before this happened or was it after?

Julie Renee: Before. I was born a clairvoyant and psychic. At age 32, I went to the Berkeley Psychic Institute. They tested me and could not figure out why all of my psychic abilities were at 100%. They asked me how I could live. They had never seen someone like me.

It was really miserable for me for about 10 years. I had information overload. On top of that, and the reason I retreated to my house was because I developed an extreme sensitivity to the environment. I was hospitalized several times for extreme allergies.

This type of overstimulation and the sensitivity go hand-in-hand with my psychic abilities. I went on disability and stayed home for a year. I spent most of my time in prayer and meditation. I had incredible insight while in my home. I was living a very inward life, then after about a year, I had gotten the message to go to India.

I went to India and it was amazing. I was recognized by all the gurus. They all knew who I was. One greeted me with, "We have been looking all over for you. I've traveled all over the planet looking for you." I needed to have that trip to remind me of who I was. It was so important to make the journey even though I knew my work was in the West.

Coni: Are there other people in your family who have this gift or are you an anomaly?

Julie Renee: I think being clairvoyant, psychic and having healing gifts runs in families. There are definite signs in my family members. One of my daughters is a healer.

Coni: When you were going through the 17 surgeries, being who you are, did you know what the outcome was going to be before the surgery?

Julie Renee: Yes, I did. I would have visions the night before the surgery of what the tumors looked like and I told the doctors about it. They would be shocked at how accurate my descriptions were.

Coni: Where were the tumors located?

Julie Renee: My thyroid had to be removed in two pieces, my cervix, my uterus, ovaries, and my fallopian tubes. There were many, many tumors on the uterus. The cervix also had tumors all over it. There was a lot of pain.

Coni: You have now worked with so many high level professionals in the area of brain regeneration. How did you happen to start working with neurosurgeons, physicists and those types of individuals?

Julie Renee: It happened organically. I left real estate in 1993 and started a massage practice and taught yoga. I had been in real estate but I knew being a real estate agent was not my calling. I needed to be in something that was very calming and soothing…somewhere I could put my hands on people.

I had this powerful energy that was flowing through my body and this was how I could give people healing energy. The practice spread like wildfire. The first week as a student, I was doing practicum and I had 18 massages.

It was like there was this message in the Universe. "Oh, there's a healer! Get over there!" I was booked nonstop with my massage practice and people spread the word that I had an extraordinary touch. It kind of morphed and after the garden experience, I developed a way to translate it and teach it to nurses and doctors.

I wrote a book called *The Divine Human Blueprint*, a 600-page manual that has just been released. It is a book on all of the steps for regeneration.

Coni: Can other people learn to do these techniques?

Julie Renee: I have a course online called the Activate Master's Program that is the basic introduction of what I do. I have taken some time off from the teaching I have been doing for the last five years to scientists, doctors and healers. I have developed a program that is designed for anyone to be able to take.

Coni: I come from a completely different background and I'm sure there are people out there with a bit of skepticism about all of this. You have a way of healing and regenerating the brain and other parts of the body. How do you explain how this really works to your clients?

Julie Renee: It actually works by using a quantum pump, so basically my hand is pumping the quantum field into this realm. We are generating a master stem cell and bringing that up to 100%. It is like in topography where a leaf is torn away but you can still see the leaf.

The blueprint for the functioning 100% master cell exists in reality. So we bring the 100% functioning master cell into physical reality. In the minor cochlea of the cell—it looks like a little caterpillar on the outside of the membrane—there is a program for regeneration. We just push on that regeneration program once we've got the master cell doing 100% and we've mirrored this master cell to this remade cell so they will breed at 100%. Then we grow a cascade of new cell growth for 110-115 days.

We need to take care once we have the regeneration. We need to tell the body that we love it and we want the brain to grow back. Therefore, no alcohol, no pain medication, which are both brain cell killers. Then drinking at least 16 4 oz. glasses of water every day will keep the brain well lubricated.

There are also brain exercises, like Lumosity or IQ programs, learning new languages...maybe a new computer program to keep the cells growing. You will start to have brain leaps. If you can get the brain leaps going for the next 110 days, you can have brain leaps for another 16 years.

Coni: How does stress affect all of this?

Julie Renee: As far as brain regeneration, stress does not stop the cells from growing. But if you're not sleeping or sleeping on high alert where you are not relaxing when you fall asleep, you're circumventing some of the cell regeneration. You only regenerate cells when you are sleeping soundly. So if you are stressed out and you are not relaxing when you sleep, you prevent the cells from regenerating.

Coni: For people that have had a dramatic Crystalline Moment in their life and are searching for something, what are some of the pearls of wisdom you can share with them?

Julie Renee: You've got to listen to that still, calm inner voice...that voice of truth that says you are greater, so much greater, than anyone has given you credit for. That you are magnificent and that you need to protect and treasure the sacred you.

That means putting yourself with people that love, nurture and care for you. And you, before you are even with those

128

people, must love, nurture and care for yourself. YOU are the one writing the script. So it is you that decides for your life.

My surviving status was the moment my doctors stopped believing in me. Maybe they never believed in me or my capacity to heal. There was a point when I went into a recovery group and they told me to stop trying so hard and give up working. That was a moment when my intuition said, these people are killing me. I ran away from them, canceled my insurance and stopped seeing medical people.

If you are just starting the journey through your Crystalline Moment, you may have six months or a year of ups and downs. I'm not saying I don't have ups and downs, but I have a specific regime. I meditate every morning, I exercise every morning. I eat well with my protein and greens in the morning. I'm setting myself up to win regardless of what's going on in my world.

****

Julie Renee's story emphasizes the importance of listening to that still inner voice and in recognizing when outside forces are not allowing you to live the life of your dreams. Whether you completely understand what she does or not, she has taken energy and healing to a whole new level.

Her important message is to remove yourself from people and circumstances that are not taking you in the direction of your dream. She is the proof that we can strive to live at 100% and that we write the script to make that happen.

She talks about how she was doing everything she knew how to do but she had not changed her mindset to do more than survive. This is once again proof that what we put out to the Universe is what we get back.

Once she changed her mindset from just surviving but living a 100% healthy life, her life changed. Did it happen overnight? No, but when you start moving in the direction of what your life is all about, looking forward and not back, you can fulfill the opportunity that your Crystalline Moment brings.

Now Julie Renee is a renowned expert on brain rejuvenation having worked with neurosurgeons, psychiatrists and other professionals in that arena. Her work includes clients such as a top-level NASA astronaut, Google VP, Pentagon officials, a United Nations Ambassador, Hollywood actors and even members of the liturgical profession.

She has written a textbook used by neurosurgeons and other professionals on brain rejuvenation. She spends her time teaching and helping people overcome all types of health, wealth and relationship issues through her work.

Julie Renee is helping hundreds of people plus contributing major research and information in the study of cell regeneration. That is no accident.

To learn more about Julie Renee and check out her programs and books, go to: www.julierenee.com.

11 5 SOUTH AFRICAN LADIES

When something devastating happens, many times we don't understand why it happened or what we are going to do while we are in the middle of whatever the situation is.

Julie Renee, as a child, may have known there was something special about her. But it was her journey from being exposed to nuclear radioactive material to becoming a brain cell regeneration expert that resulted in her awareness and living the life she was put on this earth to live. We all are put on this earth for a reason and it is our responsibility to fulfill our purpose.

This next story is not about one individual but five women who came together because they shared one common problem...their husbands all suffered from alcoholism.

I believe that the people I have had conversations with for this book came into my life for a reason. These five ladies came into my life all the way from South Africa to tell their story. They stayed in my home as guests and were a total inspiration to me.

One of the most radioactive things that can happen to any individual or family is addiction. Everyone either knows someone or themselves have suffered from this disease. It is devastating and can destroy individuals and families. But even if there is no addiction in your life, you will find lessons you can learn from the intimate conversation I had with this woman.

These five ladies all are a part of Al-Anon because their husbands were all alcoholics. When they came to visit me, they were on their way to an international Al-Anon conference in Vancouver, BC. They are spokespersons from their communities helping other families living with alcoholism.

These ladies kept me laughing the whole five magical days they stayed with me. I am grateful to them all for letting me tell their story in this book.

The one thing about people that are a part of Al-Anon as well as Alcoholics Anonymous is just that; they are anonymous so I will not be revealing the last names of these wonderful brave ladies.

Addiction is addiction, whether the addiction is alcohol, drugs, gambling, food or sex. I believe these ladies' stories will help anyone that knows someone who is suffering from some type of addiction.

****

Coni: I can't tell you how much I appreciate you allowing me to talk with you. My goal is to provide some insight to those out there that have addiction in their family.

I am certainly no expert and don't claim to have the answers, but you ladies are living it and if we can help just one person out there get the help they need, then we will have done something positive.

These types of Crystalline Moments are moments of realization that there is a problem. They are moments of clarity of the need to get out of the situation and as people will see with your stories, the moment of clarity of what Al-Anon has done for you.

But your stories go way beyond alcoholism as all of us can relate to you because we all come from families.

Nan: Before we start, I would like to say that Al-Anon is our constant and we are governed by certain traditions. We are a nonprofit organization and not aligned with any other organization.

The organization is designed to help spouses and others related to alcoholics. Even though we didn't take a drop of a drink our whole lives, we became a part of the disease. Our lives and the lives of our families were unmanageable.

Coni: Crystalline Moments is a book about people finding their way, finding the opportunities in whatever situation they find themselves. It is about the clarity of the moment of realization. As I mentioned earlier, we all know someone who suffers from alcoholism.

Nan: Yes, worldwide, it is a huge problem. Al-Anon is worldwide and there are 26,000 groups around the world. In Mexico, there are over 3,000 Al-Anon groups alone. The Al-Anon book, *One Day at a Time*, is our daily reader and is translated into over 30 different languages.

For me, 21 years ago I realized my life was on a downward spiral. At that time, I didn't realize that alcoholism was a disease. I felt he could stop whenever he needed to. I had two children and tried a lot of things on my own, but my husband could not stay sober.

I left the home a number of times and even tried blackmailing him, but nothing worked. I realized I could not continue with my life living this way. It was affecting my children very badly. It was not just because of what my husband did, but also the way that I reacted to his drinking. Every time he would drink or he would come home drunk, I would react and that would affect my children as well.

I made a decision to leave. I was set on getting a divorce. I knew if I stayed, the arguing and fighting would have a major effect on my children as they grew up. He was set in his ways but when I left that time, my husband, for the first time called Alcoholics Anonymous and started attending meetings.

We had never spoken about it but this time he knew I was serious. I was skeptical about it but decided to give it a chance. After a while, I went back to him and he told me about Al-Anon. He was going to AA but he knew Al-Anon would help me as well.

In South Africa, when you go to the meetings, they are at the same venue and time. My life changed at that moment, or as you would call it, a Crystalline Moment. When they say life begins at 40, I understand. I was close to 40 at the time and my life had a new start.

We went to meetings and we helped each other. That's what we do in our meetings. We share our experiences. The most important thing I learned from Al-Anon is that my life depends on me and my happiness is most important.

As with AA, Al-Anon focuses on the 12 steps. Al-Anon has taught me to be extremely spiritual. I have used the Al-Anon 12-step program in all aspects of my life. I've used it at work, with my kids and with my family. It is the best thing that happened to me.

Coni: Saras, how did you get involved with Al-Anon?

Saras: I've been in Al-Anon for the past 13 years. My husband hasn't walked through the doors of AA but I've got to say it's not about him. My life is about myself. I still love him dearly, but my life became a living hell.

It is about hope for people living with an alcoholic partner. People love the person and it is such a pity that they have to live with this disease. If someone you loved had cancer or another disease, you wouldn't leave them or deny the disease.

It is the same with a person suffering from alcoholism. I understand him and I have learned a lot of tolerance. It is very difficult, but I want to say that there is hope for the hopeless.

People's lives do not need to come to a standstill because there is help for everyone. We help each other.

Coni: Babs, tell me your story.

Babs: I'd like to say thank you, Coni, for this opportunity. I've been in the fellowship of Al-Anon for the past 20 years. Growing up, I had a very content life. I was the youngest, the baby. My granny had 16 children. My mother had five children. Since I was the youngest, I grew up under an umbrella. I never walked in the rain; I never did anything other children did. Other people always did for me.

I met my husband when I was 18 years old. I became a mother at 19. I was immature and childish and then we got caught in the web of alcoholism. My first life-changing moment was when I joined Al-Anon. I needed to concentrate on me and myself alone. The second moment was when I met Nan. It was my first encounter with anyone in the program and it was so life-altering.

What I have done with her by my side, I have not done with anyone else. Other life-changing moments have come by me incorporating the 12-step program into my life. I have become a wife and a mother.

I didn't know how to be or behave until I was in Al-Anon. I have to say I was so childish that when my daughter turned three, I was one. When she was four, I was two. I didn't know how to behave with an alcoholic.

I provoked everything that happened in my home. Why? Because I wanted to be more coddled. I wanted my life to be like it was before. I didn't know how to live in the house with alcoholism. I didn't know how to handle it.

Then I found Al-Anon and I'm proud to say, I work the program the way it is asked to be worked. Working it brought my husband into the fellowship. I learned to respect him from this program. After being involved in the program about 10 years, I got involved in service of the program and that grew me into someone that was much more than what I had been.

I'm in the nursing field and my hospital was not upgraded, so we didn't have computers. I knew nothing about computers but I volunteered in the Al-Anon offices and I learned how to run a computer on my own!

What this program does is give hope to the hopeless. It brings back happiness whether your partner is outside still drinking or if your partner is sober. The program asks you to focus on yourself. So if your partner does not find the fellowship, you can still be happy.

For me, I wouldn't want to do anything to change this life. The reason that after 20 years, even though my partner is sober, I am still in Al-Anon because it is an everyday living program. I have to be there so I can give hope to others the way others gave hope to me.

Coni: Thank you so much for these amazing stories. Vasie, what about you?

Vasie: Every time I hear someone from Al-Anon speak, it brings such emotion because the stories are so amazing. I also came from a large family and every Sunday, my mom would cook and everyone would come to eat.

I came from a family with lots of love. Unfortunately, my dad died when I was six and my mom died when I was 16 years old. But I was fine because I had so much love from my brothers and sisters who took care of me. I was confirmed, loved, valued and felt worthy. I was so happy with everything.

Then my husband came along. I loved everything about him. He was warm to me and I was warm to him. Everyone would say we were such a sweet couple. Slowly, I could see him drinking until the alcohol took over and it changed him and me.

I think he always drank but I loved him so much I didn't notice. As the alcohol became an element in our lives, it changed me. I was a loving, carefree kind of person, but then I became angry.

As the drinking continued, I hated this person. There was nothing I loved about him. Then slowly I started feeling sorry for myself. I used to have my own pity party all the time. I became consumed with this alcoholic in my life.

My head was him; I lost me. There was no *me* in my life. I hardly smiled and I would do crosswords so no one would talk to me. I became a completely different person.

One day when I was 8 months pregnant, I said I couldn't take it anymore. My husband would always go to the pub. I went to the hospital and I was underweight because I wouldn't eat.

The hospital asked if I could go to stay with other family members as it was not good for my pregnancy or my baby. How can I bring a child into this world, into this life? So I decided I am going to get a divorce.

I told my husband that and was going to live with my sister. When that happened, my husband hit rock bottom. It wasn't the best thing to do but I didn't understand what alcoholism was. I acted on emotions and I didn't really know what I was doing. I was feeling so sorry for myself and I did everything just for me.

After a while, my partner sought help and found AA. He would come and visit the children and me. We were like a family again so we decided to get back together.

He said he wanted to get married again on one condition. As he put the ring on my finger again, he said I want you to go to Al-Anon. I had gone to a meeting one time late at night but I thought, wait, I am trying to help you. I didn't understand that I would be helping myself.

I'm asking, why must I go to Al-Anon and solve all of these problems? So I didn't go to Al-Anon. We got married again and we were a family again but then the roller coaster started all over.

Finally, I started with Al-Anon and it became a sweet roller coaster ride. I found me again. I went to a conference and saw these other ladies that are sitting here and thought, I wish I could be like them. They looked so happy.

I was so scared and I wanted to keep it all a secret but after the years, we became great friends. We are so happy doing things together. It is God's gift to me. God said, I am going to give you these wonderful gifts, these four amazing ladies. Amazing friends!

The thing I learned is that you can't change anyone. I can only change myself and my attitude. I was so naïve to think that I could change things. We have a wonderful prayer in Al-Anon called the Serenity Prayer: *God grant me the serenity to accept things I cannot change, the courage to change the things I can, and the wisdom to know the difference.*

Look for the good things; look for the positives. Don't look at the negative. Al-Anon gave me all its tools and God. What I believed about God before was that if you do this, He will give you that.

Now I realize that you don't need to do anything. If you believe in God, he will provide. God changed my life and is always there for me. Before I always blamed God for everything in my life.

There is also a program designed for the children of alcoholics. So my husband, myself and our two children would never have gone on this journey without these programs. A lot of people have lost their partners but they still needed Al-Anon because it is not about the alcoholic. It's about your life.

It's been 20 years and I still belong to Al-Anon. I live my life the Al-Anon way. It is the new me and who I am. A good example is before I would never have worn these big gold earrings, but Al-Anon has shown me how to give myself permission to be me.

It guides me and directs me. I wish everyone had this wonderful gift.

Coni: It is a wonderful gift! Evelyn, how long have you been involved in Al-Anon?

Evelyn: I am the baby in the group. It is 10 years next year. To start, I didn't want anything to do with Al-Anon but now

I am here. I grew up in a very sheltered home. My mom was a dominating character and I didn't feel like I had a voice. I was always scared to voice an opinion or ask a question.

People from India are very protective of their children. There are lots of rules about going out and that kind of thing. Because I grew up being criticized and put down all the time, I had no self-confidence. Even in the classroom, I would sit very quietly and not ask any questions.

My biggest thing was I needed to get out. I was married when I was 21 years old. We went out, we had a good time. I loved him very much. After three years, we married and I didn't realize that for the next 10 years I was going to be married to a control freak who just took over for my mother.

Coni: You basically cut ties with your mother and are now being controlled by your husband?

Evelyn: Yes. By the first year I was married, I realized I had made a terrible mistake but it was something that I could not undo. Divorce was taboo. No one even spoke of divorce.

I talked to my mom about it but she said, "Oh no, we can't do that. What will people think?" But I saved a little money, found a cottage, got a lawyer and got divorced.

After a little while, I found my new partner. It was someone I had known for a very long time. We got together and he had the personality I was attracted to. A charming man, we had a lovely life together. He brought out something in me that allowed me to be myself.

When my son was born, he was around three or four years old when the drinking started getting out of control. It got really, really bad. I decided I'd had enough and left to stay with some friends.

We spent two months out of the house. It was difficult with three kids sharing another family's home. It was during that time that he found AA. After going on a drinking binge, he woke up and realized he had to do something about it.

The AA program is so amazing. I could see the change immediately. He asked to come back. I realized that our home was our kid's birthright. It is everything for kids to have a mom and dad.

So he would go on about Al-Anon and he got a woman to call me. She would call and call and wouldn't give up. I was getting tired of her, so eventually I agreed to go to a meeting. I was amazed as it was nothing that I was prepared for.

At the meetings, what you see in people's eyes is peace and I actually learned how to hug because I had never hugged anyone. I learned how to embrace people…even my mom!

I had regular meetings and we had home groups that we went to that I threw myself into. I've made wonderful friends like these ladies around me. I didn't think that certain things would be achievable because I didn't think I had it in me. Every time I wanted to stop, my friends would push and push.

I realized that in my life I was always stuck in co-dependent relationships. I was happy if my husband was happy. My purpose was to make sure he was happy and my children were happy. I was always looking for someone else's approval because I didn't think anyone loved me.

I realized that I needed to love myself, for me, for who I am. I didn't do that because I didn't know how. That is why I am so grateful for my friends. They love me and carried me when I didn't know how to. Al-Anon started working immediately for me.

Before I hated this man so much and I wasn't sure how I was going to ever live with him. Now we have grown together and it has taken a few years but we have jelled. It is only because of the program. Before I wasn't sure how my relationship was going to make it, but we are still happy together.

When this group of ladies started talking about this trip, I thought there is no way that this will happen. One night, I talked to my partner and I told him that I had been invited by these ladies to go on this trip and I wanted to go. He asked me how desperate I was to go. I said I was very desperate. He said, "What's stopping you?" I said, "I don't have money." He said he would buy the ticket and whatever, so go. I thank God for that. I can't believe it is happening.

It has been five days and I am so blown away. I have spent this time with four special friends. I had never left my family before and I am not spending all my time thinking about them. I am just having a ball!

Coni: I am so grateful that you allowed me to host you and get to know you. This book is about making a difference in lives and if your stories can help just one person, it will be a blessing. I don't believe in accidents. There was a reason why you contacted me. I can't wait to come to South Africa to see all of you. I love how all of you laugh together.

****

These five great ladies have so many Crystalline Moments many of us can relate to. Even if we are not married to alcoholics, we all have things in our relationships that will come up.

Whether it is our spouse or partner, our parents, our children or other family or friends, what these women talk about in their moments of clarity are things that we all can use when our Crystalline Moments provide us with opportunity.

Nan talks about leaving home several times. She talks about turning 40 and her life starting new and fresh. When someone decides to leave a home for whatever reason, that is always a Crystalline Moment. It is a moment where the opportunity is to start new.

It doesn't matter if it is because of addiction, abuse or any other reason. Stepping away from a relationship is an opportunity to look at ourselves, our values and our dreams.

All of these women have talked about discovering who they are and what they really want. It is about knowing and loving yourself. Everyone has heard the phrase, "you have to love yourself first before you can love anyone else." It is central to living the life of our dreams. We must know our purpose and understand what the vision of our dream is.

I loved when Saras talks about Al-Anon providing hope for the hopeless. We all have had times in our lives where we felt hopeless. Our Al-Anon can be the realization that we need to look at our lives and decide who we want to be.

It really boils down to the very basic idea of discovering who we are and what we want. Once we figure that out, we have hope and can move forward. Then we can reach out to others to support who we are.

Babs talks about how sheltered she was as a child and she really didn't know anything about herself until she got involved with Al-Anon. Anyone who has been protected as a child then steps out into the real world will recognize themselves in her story.

The Al-Anon principle of looking at yourself and loving who you are is also very basic to living the life of your dreams. All of these women have been able to save their marriages by discovering what makes them great.

Vasie talks about fear. When we are moving forward with the life of our dreams, it is not without fear but in the presence of fear. Fear is our partner as we step into our dream. The opportunities that come from these Crystalline Moments all came with fear. Fear is our constant companion as we move beyond the limitations of our lives.

Don't we all have doubts about what we can achieve? Evelyn learned through trusting others that anything she wants to do can be achievable. Now she has the confidence to move into her dream and be the person she wants to be.

All of these ladies talk about being grateful. Gratitude is a basic component of our journey into our destiny. Without gratitude, we will not move forward.

The Universe will not open new doors unless we show gratitude. These ladies have found abundant wonderful lives because they have been grateful for every step along the way.

12 ANN LOPER

"An Abundant Life"

Nan, Saras, Babs, Vasie and Evelyn have all had to deal with the battles of addiction. Through the help of Al-Anon, they discovered they must look at their own lives and not the lives of their alcoholic husbands.

I have talked about the loss of loved ones, of illness, of recognizing your dream, coming back from suicide, accidents and many other circumstances. There is one common theme in all of these stories: there is a life waiting for you. You just need to blueprint what that life looks like, then bridge the gap of where you are today and where you want to be. Where your dream is!

Once you have done that, you build the dream, turning that dream into your destiny.

Just like you would build a house, the first thing you do is hire an architect to design the house. You decide how many bedrooms, how many bathrooms, the floor plan and what does the kitchen look like.

It is no different in designing the life of your dreams. When Crystalline Moments happen, we may not recognize the opportunity right away, but it's the beginning of our design.

This next story is near and dear to my heart. This woman has been my best friend for over 30 years. I can tell you when I found out about her story, there was no one in more shock than I was.

When I met Ann, she was interviewing for a job that was available at an insurance office that I was a partner in. We hit it off right away, and suffice it to say that we have been through many Crystalline Moments together.

She has always been there for me and I had no idea what she had been through until several years after we became BFFs. She was always so positive, upbeat, fun and the life of the party. Tall, gorgeous and when Ann walked in the room, you could feel her presence. Everyone would turn and look.

I used to joke with her that when I was with her, no one looked down far enough to see me at 5'2". Why I decided I needed to have a 5'10" tall gorgeous best friend is beyond me, but I love her to death!

What you will find out is that looks can be deceiving. Ann suffered from abuse at the hands of her stepfather that she had hidden not just from the world, but from herself for years.

It nearly cost her life. Here is Ann's story in her own words.

****

My life began as all others on this spinning ball we humans call home – I was born! Yes, kicking and screaming, I announced my arrival on a Sunday morning in April 1952.

Did I just tell you that? Ok, so now you know I'm not a youngster, not in a midlife crisis and definitely not seen in anything that shows off my knees.

My mother and father were blissfully wed in January of that year – you can do the math. As far as I know, they never lived together afterwards, but in those days, pregnancy seemed to be a reason to get married–good or bad.

My mother was a city girl raised in Knoxville, Tennessee. She and I lived with her parents until she married my stepfather when I was still a toddler. He was a hardscrabble dirt farmer and pig raiser from Missouri, and so away we went to start this new life.

He and my mother have now both passed away, and in hindsight, I know it was never a happy marriage. I'm not even sure how they came to meet, but I don't believe it was love at first sight.

He was a dour man with a quick temper and a slow smile. I quickly became big sister to a sister and brother, and I learned just as quickly what it meant to be a "stepchild."

To say that I was raised in a dysfunctional environment would be an understatement! From an early age, my stepfather abused me emotionally, physically and later sexually. This continued until the day I left home at age 18.

If you are reading this and you have suffered the same, you know the shame, humiliation and even guilt that goes along with it. I endured all this in silence and isolation for more than 30 years. It was not a childhood I would wish on any child.

I moved to Washington, DC where I worked for the federal government and met my first husband who was a policeman. The move lasted – the marriage did not!

However, six years of marriage gave me a beautiful daughter who has been the child every parent dreams of and prays for.

After my divorce, I was alone in my life for the first time. Alone and a single mother as well! I vowed that I would never remarry, fearing that my daughter might suffer the ravages of being a stepchild.

But God and the Universe saw it another way! In 1978, I married my husband, Ed. He and I recently celebrated our 36th wedding anniversary! Courtney was only three years old when we married, so he was for all purposes, her "Dad."

He has loved her just as much as I do. I was blessed to finally find a man who truly loved me for who I am - warts and all. He has endured much with me over all these years, and I thank God for the gift he is to me.

Ed and I have moved 10 times during those 36 years, and our moves have taken us from DC to Los Angeles, CA, Portland, OR, Spartanburg, SC, Baton Rouge, LA, Atlanta, GA, Dayton, OH, and finally now back to Atlanta as we enjoy semi-retirement near our daughter, her partner and our three grandchildren.

We lived the corporate life of beautiful homes, great friends and money to spend. All these things can make you happy, but I found they brought me no joy. There was a nagging dark side within me that always wanted more or something different.

Moving was difficult but I always managed to make new friends wherever we were. Our move to Los Angeles was probably the most difficult. We were young, naïve and not prepared for the California 'scene.'

Again, God was looking out for me when he led me to a job interview at an insurance agency. There I met the woman who has been truly my best friend for more than 30 years.

Coni and I have shared every up and down and bump in the road of life that can happen, and we have remained close. We are kindred souls who share a similar childhood of difficulty and yet have come out on the light side in one piece.

We have watched our children grow up, be successful and give us grandchildren. We have watched our hair turn gray and our faces develop lines. We have been through bankruptcies, divorces, death of parents and even a spouse. We have been there for each other in spite of the many miles that keep us apart. She is my friend for life. Everyone needs a life friend, and I am thankful God sent her to me just when I needed one most.

About the time Ed and I married, I discovered – yes, that's the word I would use – wine! And, I discovered it in a big way! I had never been much of a drinker, but when I found California chardonnays, I fell in love.

Yep, head over heels in love with that cold, crisp vintage that seemed to take the edge off everything and make me happier, funnier and more relaxed than before. I now know that alcoholism is a progressive disease, and progress I did!

By 1994, I was what you would call a "big, hot mess." Although I never got a DUI, I never lost a job because of my drinking and I never killed someone on the road, I was a bona fide alcoholic.

It came to a head that summer when in the depths of depression, I attempted suicide. The darkness had finally caught me, the curtain had finally come down, and I was tired of living. I overdosed, and I came very close to succeeding. Once again, God stepped into my life (unbeknownst to me) in a huge way.

I spent more than two weeks in a mental facility where I was diagnosed as clinically depressed and a full-blown alcoholic. While I was hospitalized, that opened up my childhood that had haunted me for so many years. Through wonderful therapists, medication and a return to the simple faith of my childhood, I came out of the darkness into the light.

That has been more than 20 years ago. I have been sober since then, and I have no desire to drink.

I had spent my life in various "careers" – real estate, insurance and banking. It wasn't until 17 years ago that I finally realized my 'vocation.' I was called to serve in my local church ministering to those who have been broken just as I was broken. I found a renewed sense of purpose in helping heal broken hearts, shattered souls and abused bodies through the love God has for them.

I have a favorite passage of scripture found in the Gospel of John... *"I have come that you might have life and have it abundantly."*

It has become my life verse because it speaks to me of the difference between simply being alive and having a life that is full and joyful. It speaks to me of the difference love can make in every life and that there are so many around us who long for an abundant life when they see no hope or purpose.

And so as I write these words, I can honestly say that I have an abundant life. I am purposely grateful each day for each blessing that comes to me.

Do I have regrets? Of course. I'm human just like you. But I don't let those failures and regrets define who I am. Why? Because I don't have to.

I've made the choice to live abundantly. I pray you can too.

****

Ann spent years being ashamed of what had happened to her as a child. However, if you would have met Ann during that time, you would have thought she was the happiest, most put-together person on the planet. I never saw her down, I never saw her depressed. She was a master at disguising it. It wasn't until shortly before her attempted suicide that I had any reason to think there was anything going on.

I was living in Portland and Ann was living in Spartanburg, SC. Over the years, our telephone conversations were typical - a quick call to check in with calls lasting just a few minutes. What I started noticing is the calls were very short. She really didn't want to talk.

This went on for a few months and at first I didn't think too much of it. However, after a while I started wondering what was going on but this was Ann, bubbly, upbeat Ann. The person I had always known as a whirlwind, the life of the party. So what was going on? Little did I know what she was going through. Certainly attempted suicide was the last thing that would have ever come to my mind.

She was trying to escape from her childhood as it had finally come to roost and she was trying to handle it on her own. I had finally decided that I was going to have a conversation with her but when I would get her on the phone, it would not even be a one-minute conversation. What I didn't realize was that my dearest friend in the whole world was in trouble.

When I talked to her husband and found out what she had done, I had severe guilt for not saying something or doing something when instinctively, I felt there was something wrong. I should have been paying attention to that inner voice telling me something *more* was going on. Ann's Crystalline Moment is one that people suffering from depression and alcoholism can relate to. It is similar to Andrew's story. The difference is that an eagle saved Andrew; thank God the police got to Ann in time.

Your inner voice works not just to help and guide you but also when it comes to people you love and care about. It is important that we listen to that voice. Just like that voice can guide us into whatever life we are meant to be living, it can also let us know if we know someone in trouble.

What Ann has done with her life since has amazed me. She has made such a difference in so many other people's lives. She is just another example of what can happen when you find that opportunity...find your calling that comes from those Crystalline Moments of clarity.

If you or someone you know has not dealt with something in the past, just like with Karen and Ann, it does not go away. It will manifest itself and raise its ugly head in some other part of life. Fortunately for both of these incredible women, what they have created from their Crystalline Moments has changed not just their lives but the lives of others.

Ann now lives an amazing life in Atlanta with her wonderful husband, Ed, her daughter, Courtney, and Courtney's partner, BreeAnne, along with three incredible grandchildren. She is once again one of the most upbeat, fun people I have ever known and I am so happy and grateful she is my BFF.

13 DENISE LONES

"You are going to die if you do not get help
tonight."

As I mentioned, I felt severe guilt when I had ignored that nagging little voice that was telling me something was wrong in the conversations I'd had with Ann. Thank God she lived or I cannot even imagine the guilt I would have felt for not doing something. You are about to read Denise's story. It is a story about how that inner voice saved her life.

Denise Lones also has a very strong presence when she walks into a room. When she speaks, she is a powerful force. She knows what she wants and goes after it—someone that knows what her dream is and has embraced it. Full of vitality, she is not someone that you would ever think of as falling victim to illness.

I also met Denise through AFIRE. She trains and coaches real estate agents all over the country. She is happily married and comes from a large, strong Greek/Irish family. That explains a lot about who Denise is because her family has always been a major focus for her.

****

Coni: I have always enjoyed our conversations and you seem to be someone that recognizes when Crystalline Moments have taken place, and then you find the opportunity in them.

Denise: Some of the things that have happened throughout my life have shaped who I have become in my later years. But I will have to say there were a couple of moments that transformed how I look at everything in my life.

One of those moments was when my daughter was just a baby and a pipeline exploded in the city we were living in. A number of children died and my daughter was seriously injured. She was about a year and a half old when the accident happened. It was one of those moments when I had to face the fact that I was going to have to give up my career and take care of her. I was just so grateful she was alive.

I pretty much retired from my real estate practice to rehabilitate her. One of the things I learned is that if you have to give something up because of circumstances, if you want it back, you can always get it back. If you have it, whatever that "it" is, you will always have "it".

After my daughter's rehabilitation—she was three or three and a half, I'm sitting thinking in that moment. "Okay, I have given up a very successful real estate business. Now what?" I was a broker at the time of the accident and managing a very large real estate brokerage.

I knew I was not going to go back to managing a large real estate office. I loved what I did but knew I had to make a change. I was not ready for that kind of time and energy commitment. I still had to care for my daughter. So I had to figure out what I was going to do with my life and career.

When people have experienced really important moments in their lives, often times it's more difficult because you wonder if you can have success in any other area.

I learned from what happened to my daughter that success is not a simple formula. Success is a simple belief. For me, it was the belief that I didn't know what I was going to do exactly but I did know that whatever it was, I was going to take it on and do it well.

That is how I ended up doing what I am passionate about...helping and training others to be successful. So I went on to do coaching and training. I have had great success in that. My life was moving along very comfortably.

Throughout all my coaching and training, what I have learned and taught others is to be authentic and listen to your gut. Listen to that intuition, that inner voice, whatever it is you want to call it, that tells you when to do something or not do something. However, most of us don't listen or pay attention to what it is saying.

I have had the honor to coach and teach people to listen to those little voices that tell them they can do this or don't go near that, or that person is not the right fit for you. Whatever that voice is telling you, trust it and listen to it. It was that voice that would turn around and save my life.

My huge Crystalline Moment was when I almost died due to blood clots in my lungs. My life was good, family was good, no stress; everything was going really well. But boy, did I get smacked. It was like I was run over by a Mac truck.

I had to go in for minor outpatient surgery on both knees - really minor. I went in the morning and was out in the afternoon. I had the surgery and afterwards, I felt really great. However, when I got home, I wasn't so great because I was really groggy and sleepy. I slept for almost a day and a half. When you have knee surgery, sleeping that long is not such a great thing to do.

A few days later, I started to feel that something was wrong with me. I heard this little voice inside of me say, something is wrong, something isn't right. I called my doctor and he said it may have something to do with the painkillers I was taking. "Let's get you off the painkillers and see how you do." The next day, my voice was still telling me something was not right.

My family and I decided we were going to go to our summer home a few hours away. I could really relax and enjoy the beautiful river and our nice home there. After we arrived, we decided to spend the day on the boat, but as I stepped onto it, my intuition said, "Call the doctor. Something is not right."

I had noticed earlier that I was huffing and puffing a little bit when walking; nothing serious, but enough to take notice of.

I wasn't in any pain or discomfort. I spoke with my doctor's nurse and told her what was going on with me and that something just did not feel right. I just wanted to advise the doctor and that we were going out on the boat for the day. She thanked me for calling and would discuss my symptoms with the doctor. Then we started off down the river.

Within a few minutes, my doctor called back. "You need to turn the boat around and go immediately to the local hospital. I think you have a blood clot in your lung. I don't want you to freak out, but go to the hospital immediately." I was stunned to hear this, but we turned back and headed to the local hospital.

In the hospital's emergency room, I told them what my doctor had said and they proceeded to perform several tests. The doctor came back and told me everything checked out okay and I was cleared to go home. He told me to check in with my personal doctor in the next couple of weeks, but that I probably was suffering from the aftereffects of surgery and may just be tired.

We head back to our summer home to have a nice dinner. I walked in the front door and my intuition didn't talk to me now...it screamed that if I don't get this checked out further, I am going to die. I don't care what you call it - some people call it God, some people call it a voice - whatever you call it - I don't care what you name it. It was the loudest scream I've ever heard. There was no doubt in my mind that the presence of God was speaking to me.

I told my husband that I didn't want to frighten our daughter, but if we don't go home right now for further testing, I'm going to die. He looked at me and asked how I knew. I just replied that I knew.

He suggested we go back to the hospital we had just come from, but they had missed it the first time so I didn't want to. The drive home was horrifying because I knew I was dying. It was the longest drive I've ever had.

Coni: How far was the drive?

Denise: The drive was three hours, but I wanted to go to my own doctor where I felt safe. When we got there, my doctor said they needed to do a blood test and a Cat Scan immediately. They did the blood test that detects how your blood is clotting and they found there was a clot somewhere.

After going to a different location for the Cat Scan, two very official-looking men came out to tell my husband that they had found something. I asked them if they had found a blood clot. They looked at each other then turned to us to tell us they had found multiple blood clots in both of my lungs. They said if you don't go to the hospital right now, you are going to die. They asked if they should call an ambulance or if my husband could drive me. The hospital was only 5 minutes away, so we drove.

At the hospital, a team of doctors were waiting for us. They literally grabbed me and put me up on the gurney. Doctors and nurses were all over me trying to save my life. I had acute bilateral multiple blood clots and would have surely died if I hadn't received treatment that day. My doctor later told me that he had never seen anyone survive given the number of blood clots in my lungs.

The funny thing is while I was in the hospital, I was not afraid. I knew God was with me every step of the way and had alerted me to the seriousness of the situation. He would take care of me.

I stayed in intensive care between two and three weeks. Surprisingly enough, I didn't suffer from a lot of pain and was quite comfortable. An overwhelming sense of peace fell over me. I believed that I would not be here if I had not listened to my intuition. The doctors would tell me and my family that if one of the blood clots burst, I could still die, but I had no fear. I knew there was a greater purpose for what happened to me.

When I look back on my life and at these traumatic events, my intuition was always telling me something wasn't right. I can't count the number of times that I didn't listen. I would think, "Oh, don't be silly, you're overreacting", or, "Oh, you're just being judgmental." I think women especially play these minimizing thoughts of the "Oh, don't be silly" game.

We, as human beings, are given a gift and that is our intuition. I just want people to listen to it. When I coach or train someone, I will ask this question, "What is your biggest challenge or what are you most afraid of?' They usually will say they don't know. I will stop them right there and ask them to really think about the question I just asked and to feel it in their gut, not in their head...only from the gut this time.

Nine times out of ten, when they really start to feel their fear, they will start to cry because for once, they get in touch with their emotion. That intuition, that gut, is always there to answer your question. All you need to do is to tap into it to have the answer. If you ask yourself what you are afraid of, just stop thinking about it. Start feeling it and start trusting the answer you are getting.

Training people to learn to trust their intuition or gut feeling and then to have it come full circle, to me, is an incredible gift. My intuition that just happened to save my life has been the greatest gift I've been blessed with. I have had to learn to trust in it and listen to it without questioning it, without over-thinking it.

I tell people that we will either get better from what we have been through or we will get bitter. You have to choose to get better. You have to look at the challenges you've had in your life and ask if you have listened to that intuition or if you have fought it. You have to listen to that strong voice inside of you that is saying something is not working for you, something is out of place or out of balance. You need to turn your challenges into victories and not be a victim of it.

This experience solidified all of my life's work. It was the greatest moment of wow, my greatest Crystalline Moment. I know that I am on the right track and that this gift that I have been given needs to be shared with others. I need to train others to listen and respect that voice. Our intuition or voice is our guide, though many people look outside of themselves for a guide.

I find when I coach clients, they ask for help from me and they think that I am the one who is going to give them all the answers. My job, however, is to point that back to them and train them how to read the signals they already have.

What is your body telling you? What is your gut or your voice telling you? What does your mind already have clarity on? It's not clear when you think about it. It's only clear when you feel it. It's been a real big blessing that my intuition helped me save my life.

Coni: This is one of the common themes among all of the conversations I have done for this book. The message is to listen to that inner voice. It is so important and you certainly solidified that message in such a wonderful, eloquent way on what that really means and how important it is. It saved your life.

Denise: You are absolutely right. I've always tried to listen to that intuition but this time it was screaming, 'You are going to die if you do not get help tonight.' We were at our summer home so there were certain things we normally do before we leave. There was food on the table and things laying around and when I told my husband we had to go, he asked, "Right now?" and I replied, "Right now." It was really that powerful.

With my clients, when they really listen to their inner voice, it is phenomenal what happens. It is life-saving for them. Especially when I ask women that are working too hard, why are you working this hard? Isn't there something else in life? What's your passion? What brings you joy?

It is not about the quantity in your business; it is the quality. The money will come later if you can respect and listen to your inner voice. Your inner voice is not going to take you down the wrong road, or push you off of a cliff. It will take care of you and guide you to a safe place every time.

Coni: In my early days, I tried to argue with my inner voice and my inner voice always won!

Denise: Right! It may not win at that moment but in the end it will always win. Now, every day when I look for opportunities to guide people, even before they hire me, I listen to my intuition and the gut feeling I get working with them. If I think you are missing something or avoiding something, I have to call you on it. If you're uncomfortable with that, we can't work together.

What is really so incredible is this incident not only changed me, but my husband decided he should start listening to his inner voice as well. We are both so very thankful for it every day.

Coni: I understand you have started a special foundation?

Denise: Yes. I have become a certified grief specialist. So many people, like you, have lost their husband, wife, child or other loved person. I started this because a friend of mine lost a baby and watching the grief she went through was monumental.

With the help of another woman, we started a foundation that educates and helps people going through the grief process. Many times they don't know where to go with their grief. Many times we find that people had unfinished business with the people they have lost.

We help them find the right places in their communities to get the help that they need. We match them up with people that have been where they are now. People relate to people that have been through similar situations.

****

Is it an accident that Denise has spent her life teaching people to listen to that inner voice? You may call it God, your inner voice, your gut or your intuition. It doesn't matter what you call it, we all have it. There are no accidents, and because she had practiced listening to her intuition when she needed to hear it, her gut screamed at her.

All we have to do is ask a question and then tune in to what our inner voice is telling us to guide us in the right direction. The more we listen, the clearer that voice becomes.

I was a slow learner and would argue with that voice saying to myself, "My thinking knows better. I am not going to go that direction because my brain said go another way."

It never worked out and at times with serious consequences. It either set me up for a huge loss, either financial or personal, or I would realize I was going the wrong direction and it would be expensive in time and money to get back on track.

Each time you hear a message from your inner voice, it's a Crystalline Moment. You can either take the opportunity that is being put in front of you, like with Denise, saving her life, or you can ignore it. Now you are living your life by default rather than design.

What is core to living the life of your dreams? When I talk about living our life by design, what I am really saying is by listening to what the Universe is communicating to us through that voice. The great thing is that the more we listen, the more clarity the voice has.

Denise's foundation is called Isiah Foundation. You can find out more about it by contacting Denise personally at 360-527-8904 or by visiting her website at www.thelonesgroup.com.

14 KAREL MURRAY

"We had the perfect soap opera and look what happens"

Denise Lones lives her life listening to her inner voice and teaches others how to listen to theirs. Every time our inner voice speaks, it is a Crystalline Moment. There is a choice and opportunity. We can go with our inner voice or our thinking.

This may be just a small decision that we need to make or it could be a life-changing moment like the one Denise had. Even those things that seem to be insignificant when our little voice speaks up has some sort of importance and needs to be listened to. We may not understand why at the moment but there is a reason.

Karel created a career with her great sense of humor but humor with a message. Karel's view of the world is from a filter where she sees things by looking through a laughter telescope.

She describes herself as a Motivational Humorist, business strategy consultant and author. I describe her as one of the funniest people I have met with a great message.

Her website, karelmurray.com, talks about the presentations she does both nationally and internationally, and how people will understand the five points she makes when they hire her to speak.

Her first point is, "I bring a 'nothing but the truth' humorous and insightful approach to presentations which are solidly based on business strategy and practical life applications."

That really does also describe what I have observed of her. Her practical life advice fits right in with the Crystalline Moments we have been talking about in this book. This story shows how humor helped through a difficult time and how her Crystalline Moments helped move her forward.

This particular event happened when Karel was only 25 years old. She was married with a six month-old child. I am sharing an excerpt from her book entitled, *Hitting our Stride*, to tell her story. You will smile!

****

One moment I'm playing softball with a highly skilled team of women on a 95-degree sunny day. The next, I'm lying in a hospital bed. My body refused to respond to mental commands and the left side of my face appeared to have melted, drooping towards my shoulder.

170

Unable to connect my thoughts enough to speak, the few words that did escape sounded like slurred soft mumbles. Vertigo and nausea a constant companion, I had trouble navigating the eating process.

Strangely enough, I had no concern at all about my condition. My gaze took in the soulful and scared expression of my husband, Rick, while he comforted our six-month-old son near the side of my bed. My heart felt heavy with unbelievable regret; images of all the times I hadn't told Rick I loved him, how I fumbled with motherly duties, and the absence of our own family traditions.

Thoughts of extreme disappointment at the lack of a meaningful relationship with my parents dominated my conscious hours. As far as I knew, at the age of 25, I would be wheelchair-bound, unable to feed myself or hold a conversation again. And yet, regret weighed more heavily on me than thoughts about what I wouldn't be able to do in the future.

Suddenly, the hospital privacy curtain whipped to the side and a cherubic face peered at the three of us. An older heavy woman with frizzy gray hair, a moon-shaped face, wearing a gray volunteer uniform, leaned towards my husband and stated, "What? Tragedy? No time for that! I know exactly what you need!"

She twirled around, her white orthopedic shoes squeaking on the linoleum, and reached into a metal cart positioned in the doorway.

With unbelievable adeptness, she returned to the bedside and shoved a *Sports Illustrated* magazine in Rick's unoccupied hand and announced, "No time to wallow in sadness. Read! Read and rejoin what is happening in the world!"

Even though my face couldn't register my emotions, I laughed so hard internally I thought I might cut off my air supply. I know my eyes sparkled with delight at seeing the expression on Rick's face and our son, Ben's fascination with this wild woman.

Almost as if she heard me, her head swiveled toward me and understanding showed in her ruddy features. The volunteer whisked out a Baby Ruth candy bar from her front pocket and tore off the top half of the wrapper. With a quick smile, she bent forward and shoved the candy into my half-opened mouth, lodging it securely against my teeth. She held my chin and said, "Everything is better with candy! Sweetness in your life…nothing like it!" My husband's abrupt laugh at the sight is something I remember to this day for the sheer joy of the sound.

The gray lady raised her hands chest high, palms outward and said softy, with unparalleled love, "There is always hope and possibility. Get on with life." Winking, she spun around, grabbed the cart handle and moved quickly around the corner into the hospital corridor.

I looked back at my husband only to see him shaking his head and watched a broad, knowing smile spread on his lips. Rick exclaimed loudly, "We can't even do this hospital scene right! We had the perfect soap opera and look what happens!" He tossed his head back and laughed loudly and fully.

It is my belief that our guardian angel visited us that day. In what seemed our darkest moment, her ray of hope gave Rick the strength to deal with a newborn baby and a potentially crippled wife, while it gave me a true chance for personal happiness and emotional calm.

At that moment, I knew that what I did in the future had nothing to do with my past. I could write my life story any way I wanted. Unable to express verbally these thoughts to those who loved me most, I realized I had to prepare to do battle within myself to solve the issues, real and imagined.

The clinical diagnosis began as Multiple Sclerosis, then we learned that medications used to treat MS created stroke-like symptoms for me. Once they discontinued the prescribed drugs, I began to get better.

My face returned to the proper symmetry and the numbness in my left side began to fade. I finally held my son without supervision after 12 weeks; a milestone of such magnitude that nothing compares. Years later, the Mayo Clinic ruled out the original diagnosis and determined that issues related to my childhood's deadly bout with measles had damaged a few nerves in the brain and they prescribed a medical regimen that gave me my life back.

In those months of silence, trapped in a body that wouldn't cooperate, I waged an internal war that not only made me stronger but allowed me to recognize an essential truth in life that regret is a powerful emotional detriment.

My mother's effort at raising me may have included conflicting messages, but I learned that life is messy. Sometimes we get it right on the first try and other times we struggle, never quite making contact when it counts the most. At least she tried to pass on her wisdom.

In order to keep focused about my own personal responsibility, I've developed a reality checklist in terms of essential truths. It's what keeps me honest, and it is the list by which I guide my life. I want to share it with you because it took a dramatic event before I finally understood how precious life was. I hit a brick wall rather than hitting my stride. I hope through collective insight we can skirt around the obstacles and anticipate change while welcoming with open arms whatever comes into our lives.

Information turned into wisdom has incredible healing power. Perhaps some of these truths will hit home for you and others may be your wake-up call. I ask that you consider your own personal truth.

Know that whatever it is, it's worth adding to the chorus of female voices as we announce to the world in the words of Helen Reddy, "We are women…hear us roar!"

Reality Checklist of Ten Essential Truths

1. You are not the center of the Universe but part of a greater collective humanity. What hurts others ultimately harms you.
2. Your actions and words impact others. Try to take complete responsibility for how you interact with people and the decisions you make. Once that happens, I believe we are set free to live an unhampered life.
3. You are not inconsequential; you matter to yourself and to those who truly love you for who you are. With that strength of personal commitment, you show your children the path to their own strength.
4. The past can't be changed. You are a brand new person each day that you wake up. The experiences for the current moment mold you so you can face the challenges of the next day. Everything that happens to you has a purpose. It's up to you to learn the lesson and move on.
5. Create opportunity by the attitude you wear.
6. Earn the right to be part of someone's life. Don't suffer entitlement attitudes. Provide good and fair exchanges of personal value and then hope that your offering is recognized and access to friendship is returned. In the converse, people need to earn the right to be part of your life. There are throngs of individuals who shine in their love of others and ethical beliefs. It makes great sense not to make room for harmful, toxic people in your life, ever.
7. Refuse to be a victim of circumstance or any career situation. Set your path by the decisions you make and the personal ethics you hold. Don't fear vicious personalities; try to discover what made them that way and gain an understanding for what motives them. Acknowledge the behavior and move on.

8. Seek perspective and work continually not to be wounded by toxic people who take joy in dishing out cruelties. Looking for the source of an attack may reveal a perceived slight, professional jealousy, or something that has absolutely nothing to do with you. Keeping a personal distance and not reacting before you fully understand the dimensions of the conflict can prove to be a wise course of action.

9. Don't apologize for your personal idiosyncrasies. Whistle softly while you shop, sing opera in the car, stop and make chattering noises at squirrels, or tear up at a movie trailer. If they are going to love you, they have to love all of you.

10. Let emotional calm rule when chaos surrounds you. When people are counting on you to have emotional balance, step back, observe and react to accurate information. Then, after a highly charged event, get through the hyperventilation or tears in private. Just like the commercial says, "Never let them see you sweat."

I'm a fatalist and I believe things happen for a reason and that people enter our lives when we most need them, even if we don't understand why they are there. I've experienced intense connections with people for no obvious reason, but it eventually is revealed they either have something to teach me or I am there to help them.

Try to accept your personal journey for what it is: an opportunity to grow into the ultimate person you're supposed to be.

****

This is just one of Karel's great stories but this speaks to everything we have been talking about—the opportunity that Crystalline Moments offer and how they are a part of our blueprint to living the life of our dreams.

When Karel was unable to speak lying in a hospital bed, thoughts went to regret for not telling her husband she loved him more often. Denise Lones mentions that one of the things she finds through her foundation is that people who have lost loved ones often times have unfinished business with the people they have lost.

She also talks about the regrets she had with not having family traditions and the lack of a meaningful relationship with her parents.

The good news is she is alive and thank goodness she's now well enough to tell her husband she loves him and can change the relationships in her life that she had regrets about. It gave her the realization that we need to cherish and honor the relationships in our lives.

Is there someone in your life you need to have a conversation with or tell them that you love them? In order to move into the life of our dreams, we must look at our relationships and find a way to put that area of our life in alignment with our dreams.

For Karel, that was the acorn that was planted to later grow into the giant oak tree of her legacy of books and teachings. She talks about how things happen for a reason. What seemed like a tragic thing that happened to her at such a young age turned out to be a great gift!

Before the volunteer came into the room, Rick was scared and worried. Karel was thinking about the fact that she may never walk again. The volunteer changed the perception of their situation for both Karel and Rick.

That is a very valuable lesson in bridging the gap of the life we are living to the life of our dreams. The problem is not the problem; the problem is the perception of the problem. With Karel and Rick now unstuck from their circumstances and conditions, they opened themselves up to the opportunities that this Crystalline Moment was bringing.

Wouldn't it be great if we all could have a frizzy, gray-haired lady come and interrupt our thought patterns when necessary? The good news is we really do. We can all do a pattern interrupt when we realize we're off track and not in alignment.

When I am coaching, I tell people to imagine they have a large red button or draw a large button with the word "pause" on it. When you recognize that your thoughts are not in alignment, you hit your pause button and say stop or pause.

Follow it up with a statement or affirmation that will put you back in alignment with the energy of the opportunity you have in front of you. That is what the volunteer, or as Karel called her, guardian angel, did for her and Rick.

Let's examine Karel's checklist. Each of the 10 points represents some very important lessons that we all need to live by to have the lives of our dreams. How we see and express ourselves will reflect out to the Universe and that is what the Universe will give us more of.

As Karel stated, we all are connected energetically. Not only are we connected with one another, but with all things in this Universe at a molecular level. That is why we can create new brain cells as Julie Renee talks about. We can manifest what we want in our lives if we live our life in the moment, with purpose and with a clear vision of what our dreams are.

We all have said or done something we regret. In order for you to move into the higher frequency of living the life of your dreams, you must resolve what has happened - not for the sake of the other person, but for the sake of your own life and dream. If someone has harmed you, you must forgive them and find a way to wish them well. It is for the good of you, not for them.

Some of us when we have a Crystalline Moment start looking at the opportunities we see. But then, immediately after, we have doubts about our deserving that opportunity. However, we all can move forward toward the opportunity either through longing or discontent.

We allow our longings and discontent to be our guides. In living our lives this way, we teach our children how to listen and observe the longings and discontentment in their lives.

If we live our lives using these guides and observing what opportunities are possible based on each Crystalline Moment, we then will grow and expand as our dreams reveal themselves to us.

It's like climbing that mountain where we cannot see what is on the other side until we reach the top. Each opportunity we grasp is one step closer to the top and revealing all that our dreams hold for us.

179

15 MARY MORRISSEY

"Notice what you are noticing"

Karel is wonderfully inspirational and has helped thousands through speaking, consulting, blogging and books. I love her because she does it with such incredible humor.

We all can learn from others because everyone we cross paths with has a purpose in our lives. I have had the great fortune to have met some amazing people in my life as is evident by this book.

Mary Morrissey has been my teacher for many years. I have followed her life, I went to her church and now because of her organization, I am a Life Mastery Consultant. I think you could say she has had a bit of influence on my life. I became a much more spiritual person when I found what I was looking for in her teachings.

I had become disillusioned with religion and had walked away from my Catholic upbringing but always was in search of something. For many years, I didn't know what that *something* was.

While my daughter, Sherrie and I were living in Portland, OR, we talked about the fact that we needed something more in our lives. We attended a few different denominational churches but hadn't found the ONE.

Sherrie heard about a church that was meeting in a movie theater. She attended a few times and told me that she thought this was exactly what she was looking for and that I needed to check it out.

The first Sunday there hooked me on Mary Morrissey and her teachings. I traveled constantly around the country so I couldn't attend services every Sunday, but when I was in town, I would be there. Mary talked about universal laws, quantum fields and energy and how they worked in our daily lives. She had studied all of the different belief systems and would bring speakers to the church, all experts from these fields of study. I particularly remember when, not long after 911, she invited an Imam, a spiritual leader in the Muslim community, to speak at Sunday services.

Mary experienced more than one Crystalline Moment in her life but I am going to share just one. This is a story we can all learn from.

Mary has a Master's degree in Counseling Psychology and an honorary doctorate in Humane Letters. Her academic work included studying the Universal Laws for many years and she wanted to teach others. Mary decided she wanted to travel around the country, so she and her husband leased out the blueberry farm they owned and rented out their house.

After putting all of their belongings into storage, they paid off their car including other debts and bought everything they needed to give them the freedom to travel for a year. Her husband purchased window washing equipment so he could earn extra money should they need it along their travels. They started out on their trip with $300 in their pocket and stepped out in faith that everything would work.

The trip turned out to be as much about Mary learning how to create abundance as much as it was about teaching others. At one point, they were down to $3 and in a low income, high crime area in Florida where there weren't a lot of people wanting their windows washed. At first, she said okay, I could call family and ask them to send some money, but then realized that somehow she was out of alignment with the Law of Abundance.

Once she was able to align herself with the revelation that she was giving of her time and teaching but not her money, she decided she needed to start tithing. From the $3 they had, she gave 30 cents to a small church in Florida. Moving forward, their opportunities continued to grow and with the help of her husband's small window washing business, they were able to continue traveling the remainder of the year.

From that humble beginning, her following continued to grow and when they returned to Oregon a year later, they started the Living Enrichment Center. The church began in their farmhouse with about a dozen people. When I joined at the movie theater, the fellowship had grown to a few hundred.

Her reputation of being an outstanding teacher grew more and so did her church—so much that the church purchased a 95-acre campus that housed a 90,000+ square foot building, a retreat center, a school, a bookstore, a restaurant and a television station. Mary would invite friends, people like Bob Proctor, Deepak Chopra and Dr. Wayne Dyer to come and present at the church. Popular musicians at the time, such as Kenny Loggins, would come to sing.

Her ministries soon went global. She spoke at the United Nations three times, and facilitated weeklong meetings with His Holiness The Dalai Lama. She met with Nelson Mandela in Cape Town, South Africa to address the most significant issues the world faced at the time. She wrote three books, one of which was turned into a PBS movie.

During this timeframe, she remarried and her new husband took over their personal finances as well as overseeing the church finances. Her worldwide travels meant being gone for extended periods of time until her father became ill and passed. It was then that she came home and stayed for eight weeks.

These are her words of what happened:

"During the next eight weeks, I started to open some mail. I began to discover some things about the financial management of my life and my work. What I would ultimately unearth over time would be devastating to me.

It was simply a misappropriation of funds, called co-mingling. It was all of the things that you would absolutely never want to have happen. It would lead me down a path where I needed to have the man I had been married to placed in a mental institution, and ultimately he would go to prison.

Meanwhile, my marriage would dissolve. It by far was the darkest 'night' of my life. I had never ever known such darkness. I didn't know how I was going to survive. But I distinctly remember the moment when I made the decision that I was going to survive it."

Her Crystalline Moment is defined behind the thought of, "I don't know how I am going to survive this." As a *trained observer**, Mary chose the decision to survive when after a thorough investigation, officials brought charges of financial co-mingling against her husband. He spent a year in a mental hospital and a year in prison, a sad testament to the power of mental illness misdiagnosis. Her church board, nor Mary, were ever charged with anything and exonerated of any wrongdoing in the mid 2000's.

*We all need to be *"trained observers"* of our lives.

Here is an assessment of a trained observer:

A *trained observer* possesses the ability to see and be aware of the differences between and among various things, situations, people and forms of any kind. It is the ability to notice the obvious, which is not always obvious to everyone else. In other words, *"notice what you are noticing"*.

All of us have an observer that can stop our thoughts and replace them with a decision that matches our dream frequency. Notice what you are saying to yourself, or as Mary would say: "notice what you are noticing" as she did. She followed, "I don't know how I am going to survive" with, "Well, that is not an empowering thought." She then followed that thought with another that was in alignment with her life.

Here is how Mary describes it:

"Then it was like, okay, no matter how this comes down, I know my truth. I know what I was a part of. I know what I *thought* was happening, and I had to get down to that center point.

Meanwhile, there was a moment when I woke up and I am watching everything I had built fall apart. The first thought that hit my consciousness was, I am not going to be able to handle this pressure. Right behind that thought, I hear, "That's not a very empowering thought."

I say back to that part, little Self to big Self—help! I need a better thought. And immediately, it says, "Ask and you shall be given."

Ask yourself, what could I do here? You need to ask some bigger questions.

So I said, I need a new thought then. And immediately, what landed in my consciousness was this:

I remembered being in junior high school and learning that on every square inch of the human body there are 14.7 pounds of atmospheric pressure per square inch of skin pressing in. The average woman has 3,000 pounds of atmospheric pressure on her. The average man has 4,000 pounds of atmospheric pressure on him. But because of the system, we are divinely designed. Our bodies have 14.7 pounds of atmospheric pressure per square inch from the circulatory system, from the muscles, from the bones, from the organs pressing out.

This is called stasis, or balance. You did not wake up this morning and get up and say, "Boy, I sure hope I don't get flattened today by all that atmospheric pressure on my face!" Nor did you think, "Well, I hope I don't explode from all the pressure I'm going to exert." You never thought about it because there's balance.

Well, that is what came to me. My first thought was, I'm not going to be able to handle the pressure. Then I realized when there's internal pressure equal to the external pressure, again, you have balance.

I'm saying now, this looks bigger than I feel and then what I know how to handle. This looks very scary to me. What's going to happen here?

***That's* the perfect moment for deepening and expansion of you. That is a Crystalline Moment!"**

****

I was attending Mary's church while all of this was happening. It made the newspapers and TV news. People questioned her and her teachings. How could she not know and what can we believe or not believe? I am sure my feelings were the same as many others. *How can this be?*

Mary's 20+ years of teaching was now in question and even while she doubted what her own future held and whether she would survive, I continued to go to a temporary church set

187

up by a group of the church leaders. I personally still believed in what she had taught.

I now know that her Crystalline Moment of knowing she was going to be okay is the same as all of our moments. Once we make the decision to stop and observe what we're thinking and doing, we can then change the alignment of our thoughts to match our dreams. It is about interrupting our thought pattern like the nurse did for Karel and Rick. When we ask ourselves the right questions, the next step will become apparent. We then start seeing what the Universe has in store for us. There is a purposeful reason why these things are placed in front of us.

I love a quote I have heard Oprah say many times:

"First, the Universe will hit you with a pebble. If you don't listen to that inner voice, then it's a stone, then a boulder and if that doesn't work, a brick wall!"

Mary had hit her brick wall and there was something bigger the Universe had in mind for her. Shortly after the church fell apart, Mary sent out an email asking if people in the congregation would like to receive daily inspirational messages from her. I signed up after the first email I received. Regardless of what happened to Mary, she was a great teacher.

I have been receiving her daily messages ever since. What Mary didn't know, and none of us do when these moments happen to us, is what will happen next.

Mary knew she still wanted to teach. She started inviting people to talks in Portland, Seattle and Los Angeles where she would continue to teach what she knew for sure...that the Universe provides for those who believe.

Ultimately, Mary started a company called Life Mastery Institute and now has taught hundreds of like-minded people from all around the globe how to live the lives of their dreams.

As I mentioned in the beginning, to say that her teachings have been instrumental in my own life and Crystalline Moments is an understatement. Her teachings helped me get through the death of my husband and find the opportunities that my "moment" had brought to me. To learn more about Mary, please visit her website at www.marymorrissey.com.

Even if the Crystalline Moment is something positive, we don't always see the opportunity which is the real outcome. We may think it is one thing when it is something quite different.

When Donna Mikkin talks about her and her husband winning the $34.5 million New York State Lottery, it took her several years to figure out that the money was not the opportunity. The opportunity would come when she realized that she was able to teach real estate agents how to be the best in their field, and that she could do it from abundance rather than from shortage.

The lessons we learn from these amazing stories can be used when those "moments" show up in our own lives.

Each of these stories have given us a way to explore opportunities and what the Universe is holding for us.

16 TAYLOR WILLIAMS

"You are extraordinary"

Earlier I told you the story about my granddaughter, Kenzie, and what an amazing future she has as a fashion designer. The good news is I am not going to bore you with stories about all nine of my grandchildren, but I am going to introduce you to one more.

I saved her story for the last story in this book for a very good reason. To say that I have been inspired by Taylor and Kenzie is a gross understatement. When you hear Taylor's story, I am sure you will understand.

Taylor is 15 as of this writing, but her story starts when she celebrated her eighth birthday. Her giving back started way before that with food drives that were combined with her birthday for as long as I can remember. Taylor is an extremely bright young lady and is wise way beyond her years.

At 12 years old, Taylor started writing a blog while working toward her 2nd degree black belt for mixed martial arts. She sounded like she was an ancient Greek philosopher rather than a 12 year-old!

What Taylor has accomplished in her young years, most adults will never accomplish in their lifetime—everything from collecting stuffed animals for police to helping build water wells in both Africa and Haiti. I'm sure she's just getting warmed up.

Here is one sample from her blogs:

"No machine can do the work of extraordinary people."

This is what a clever man once told me. Ordinary people's work is equal to that of a programmed machine whereas extraordinary work has no synonym of equal value.

Nothing can compare with something extraordinary because it is genuine and comes from one person. I was 7 years old when SBN Dan (then, BSBN) gave me a picture with this message written on it. The last line of his wisdom stated, "you are extraordinary."

I didn't fully understand the message until my first black belt test in 2009. Then and now, it has made me realize that normal or ordinary never achieves anything more than typical. Be extraordinary and do great things! Make this black belt test the best it can be and always work at a higher level than any machine.

For the last (black belt) phase, I have gotten rather behind on my requirements. As well as making excuses to myself about why I didn't push harder. Then today, something clicked again and I've already done 1,000 quality sit-ups.

A certain memory is what drove me out of my little train of thought. It was from June 27, 2009 - almost 2 years ago at the Power Within fire walk in Sandy, Oregon. We all had had a tough day and the actual fire walking was yet to begin.

Everybody was given an arrow that represented an obstacle that we had to break (literally) through. When it was my turn, I promised myself I would never make excuses for things in my control. I still have that arrow, it is in two pieces now and my mental outlook to finish all requirements in the given time has not only been rekindled but is now roaring with an intense desire to succeed.

These two philosophies will stay with me for the rest of my life."

Taylor started Mixed Martial Arts Program with her family when she was six years old. She is now 15 and has soared into becoming one of the superstars at Aim High Academy of Martial Arts. She's an amazing instructor and part of the staff.

Taylor was recently interviewed in a podcast for Aim High and was so eloquent that I wanted to use portions of the interview here.

When Taylor was very young, she started incorporating food drives in with her birthdays. You could give her a birthday present but you would also donate cans of food. When I asked her what she got out of doing this she told me, "I loved to see them smile."

When she turned eight, she wanted to collect teddy bears for the police to carry in their cars to give to children they encountered. Here is what she said:

"I had to do a project and I wanted to collect teddy bears for the police. I had heard stories about when the police are called to a location and there are scared kids, the police will give them a stuffed animal to help calm them down and make them feel safe.

I thought it was really cool, so since I already had so much, I wanted to give and be able to donate some of my toys. Then I got my friends to do the same and we spread the word. We ended up donating 200 bears to the police department. That was pretty awesome!"

Taylor started working on her 1st degree black belt when she was nine years old. She would complete it when she turned 10. A year later, she did her first water well project. One out of nine people in the world do not have clean drinking water.

"When I was nine, I saw that other people were doing projects so I decided to do one too. I looked around at projects and there were lots of food drives going on so I wanted to do something different. At that time, I didn't really know about the problems with people having clean water. I found a charity called Water First International and I was able to raise money through my community.

We raised enough money to purchase a water pump in Bangladesh and a small well in Ethiopia with each servicing over 100 people. Before this, people had to walk six miles each day for dirty water and I felt really good about helping them get clean water."

When I asked her, what would you say the biggest gift is in working on projects like this? She replied again, "I love it when I get to see them smile." How many of us do something of this magnitude just to see someone smile?

When Taylor was eight years old, after one of her classes, she decided her goal was to be a 3rd degree black belt before she got out of high school. In the podcast, she was asked what motivated her. "I'm inspired by all of the amazing instructors around me. I don't want to just achieve and be mediocre."

Now 15, Taylor is currently in training for her 3rd degree belt.

"It is challenging and everyone is there to support you," she said about her experience. "They are not going to hold you any lower than what they know you can do."

Taylor has been an instructor at Aim High for three years and was helping out with classes even before that. She learns as much from the students as they learn from her. Isn't that a life lesson we often have when we give back in some way? We always receive more than what we give.

When asked if martial arts has been easy, she replied:

"No, but it's been wonderful with all of the challenges. When I was nine, I was asked to be part of the Power Within team to get my 1st degree black belt. Originally, I was supposed to go for my candidate belt because I was a little behind the others since I started a few months after they did. But I kept working hard and caught up. It clicked when it started getting real and intense. More like a lifestyle rather than just a hobby."

When she was asked which belt was harder, the 1st degree or 2nd degree, this is what she had to say:

"They each were difficult in different ways. The first degree test was more about learning the project management, learning the skills, and making sure I knew everything. And especially working through nerves, which was something I had a problem with. My second degree was more about learning how to be a leader in the community and branching out. That was when I started working more as an instructor. I helped out with classes but I hadn't been able to be in charge of a group of people."

In the podcast, the comment was made that a lot of kids who are 14 "won't lift a finger to take out the trash", and Taylor had already impacted over 200 kids in her community and impacted hundreds of families internationally.

She was asked if this was something that her parents were helping her to do.

"It has been me that has been leading it but my parents have always helped with giving me ideas for projects and their support is always with me. I am the one that does most of the work with fundraising and getting the word out, but they are always there to help me and give me support and to help get the message out."

Taylor also developed a nutrition bar as her science fair project.

"I wanted to do something that tied back to my philanthropic works so I decided to use my knowledge in health and nutrition to come up with a solution to world hunger. When kids are suffering from severe acute malnutrition, it depletes their body and allows bacteria to invade. There are several harmful diseases that can result from that. They can include death or chronic pain and I created a supplement bar similar to an energy bar, but it replaces a meal with all the vitamins you need plus fatty acids to help rebuild the body that has been suffering from malnutrition. It proved successful for children and adults so it can service people of all ages; most especially people in undeveloped countries."

Her motivation came from seeing the results of the water well for the school in Haiti. They had sent a video and she was able to see how happy the kids were. It made her want to do more.

"I wanted to branch out my horizons. I wanted to move on from clean water to work on hunger as well."

Now she is working on her third degree black belt project as her Ethos project. After witnessing bullying in the public school system, Taylor feels that the problem is getting worse, especially with the development of technology and cyber bullying.

"As a student, I hear about things that teachers and counselors don't know about. We started an anti-bullying campaign from the point of view of students for students. We made three pamphlets; one for elementary students that's more of a picture book. It explains what a bully really is, how a bully makes the victim feel and what bystanders can do. You don't have to necessarily step in front of someone and take a punch. You can go tell a counselor. Or you can comfort the victim when it is over and make a difference that way."

Taylor's other two pamphlets address specific problems for middle school and high school students because bullying changes as age progresses. Cyber bullying or social bullying are much more common at that level.

"You can't just sit back. It has to be part of a community effort."

When asked whether she would recommend starting martial arts for other young people, she replied:

"Yes, of course, I would recommend someone start martial arts because it really does improve all aspects of your life. It makes you feel great beyond just the physical conditioning. It will help shape your lifestyle and improve your school performance. It also helps you plan for the rest of your life so you are able to live a happier life. Starting as an adult is fine as well for shaping your lifestyle."

I asked her, what was she most grateful for, and any advice she could give to parents or others to create the life they want to live.

"I'm grateful for my support team, my family and my Aim High family because they hold me to high standards but are always there to help and encourage me."

Her best advice: "Don't give up!"

****

Three simple but powerful words! I don't even know where to begin with what Taylor has achieved in 15 short years. She is a wonderful example of having Crystalline Moments and it is in her DNA to move forward with the opportunity they provide. She talks about moving from providing clean water in underdeveloped countries to solving world hunger like it is something everyone is doing every day.

The opportunities that she has embraced through her martial arts and school careers are great examples of what can happen when we seize the opportunity of those moments of clarity.

If a young girl can help a school of 500 children, or a village in Ethiopia have clean water and find a solution to help children and adults suffering from hunger, what is it you would like to achieve? What is your dream? It is never too late.

When Mary Morrissey's mother turned 90, she wrote a book and we are constantly seeing people on TV in their 70's up to even 100+ doing amazing things. We all have our story, and from our story we have Crystalline Moments that can provide us with the opportunities if we recognize them, to achieve and exceed. To become extraordinary!

We all can do little things that will help someone else less fortunate and what we will get in return is so much greater than we ever give. For example, a certain Starbucks coffee house holds the record for the number of people paying it forward by buying drinks for the people behind them. We don't have to set out to save the world like Taylor, but every little thing we do shows that we are grateful and the Universe will take notice.

For me, Taylor and Kenzie are both examples of not just really inspirational young ladies, but a lesson in gratitude. First and foremost, my gratitude for having such amazing grandchildren and gratitude to my son, Steve and daughter-in-law, Molly, for raising such intelligent, caring and inspirational children as these two. I am so grateful for the lessons that I can learn and grow with through this family.

Gratitude is an important component of living the life of your dreams. There are three major components that must be a part of the journey. The first is that in the presence of fear, you move forward. The second is forgiveness, because without blessing those who we have had discord with, we cannot step into our dream. The third is gratitude. Without gratitude, the Universe will not show you the next step to the top of your mountain, your dream.

Taylor talks about always wanting to not just achieve and be mediocre but wanting to exceed her goals. When we envision our dreams and write them down, we should always start with, "I am so happy and grateful that..." And we should always end with, "...this or something more". Remember, the Universe may have something far greater in mind for us than what we can even imagine for ourselves.

Taylor has far surpassed what many of us will do in a lifetime and I cannot wait to see where she soars to next.

And YES, this grandmother is very proud!!

What We Have Learned

I, first and foremost, want to say thank you to the amazing people that were willing to share their stories with me. It takes bravery to open yourself up and be willing to share things that have changed our lives, especially if it entails pain or hurt. The one thing I realized when I was writing this is that I know some *amazing* people. What is interesting is that I have many more incredible stories left that I can share in future books. So stay tuned!

So what have we learned and what can we use as takeaways to help us in our own lives? Let's recap what we have talked about.

First and foremost, Crystalline Moments do not need to be major events. They can also be thoughts that we have had which are still crystal clear to us, even if we had them when we were a child.

What memories do you have that you can remember the details just like it was yesterday? Take a look at those memories, and see what Crystalline Moment opportunities are in those memories that may be affecting how you are living your life today. Are you living your life by design or by default, and what role do those moments have in what is happening in your life?

The moments when I was 10 have played a huge role in my life for 55 years. Now that I recognize my paradigms, I can stop, notice what I am noticing and shift my thoughts so that they fit into the design I have for my life now.

If the Crystalline Moments are ones that resulted from the loss of a loved one, what can we do to take that moment and find the opportunity to honor that person? The one thing I can say about people like Ginny and others that have moved through great loss is that the operative word is "move".

Everyone that I have talked to about the loss of loved ones that are moving forward have found some way to make a difference in other people's lives. It is a way for us to honor our loved ones and it doesn't have to be as big as what Ginny and her husband have created. It can be just performing random acts of kindness. Then in that moment, give honor to the person you have lost.

Those small little acts will accumulate and add up to us being able to smile and see joy when we think of our loved one. Some examples could be joining a support group to help others, delivering meals to seniors, or helping out at a shelter. Or think big and start a foundation; whatever feels right to you.

When you see the opportunity in that moment of clarity, the life you are to be living will start to unfold. There may be several Crystalline Moments through a series of events that will reveal the direction you are meant to be headed in. It took several Crystalline Moments for me to discover my life as a Life Mastery Consultant.

If someone gets stuck, which is why you see so many spouses who pass soon after their partner dies, it is because they cannot see the baby steps toward the opportunity. Ginny talks about pushing yourself physically. She talks about finding some sort of physical activity like running, walking or things like yoga so we can heal our mental and emotional health.

It is also important for people not to isolate themselves because then they dwell in the world of the 'whys' which only keeps them stuck. Why did this happen? Why me? Why them? When we isolate ourselves, we will not find the "what's". What is our purpose? What is next? What would I love to do? What is the opportunity?

When we are grieving, we are all different; we all grieve in our own way. For family and friends that are trying to support someone who is grieving, it is important to recognize that fact. As the person grieving, we do want family and friends to support us in ways that we need to be supported. We can do that by expressing what we need and letting people know what we need most.

Bernice Ross is one of the persons who helped me the most when Tom first passed. Her work as a psychologist and volunteer at an AIDS Clinic and working with families losing loved ones gave her a lot of insight into what helps and what doesn't. One of the things she told me is that people will want to share their stories about the loss of their loved ones. She said that it is important to not listen to those stories because they are not *your* story. I think that is great advice.

Ginny talks about how important it was to save her marriage to allow her husband to grieve in his own way while she grieved in hers. When we hear other people's stories of loss, we may think that is what we're supposed to be thinking or doing.

That is not to suggest that when we are ready to attend a support group, we shouldn't listen or share our stories, but in the days following a loss, it is best to find our own path. People want to help and the best way to do that is by listening and offering support to the person grieving.

That support can create Crystalline Moments in themselves, opportunities to think about their own lives and question whether they are living their life's purpose. We all have 525,600 minutes in a year if we are lucky enough to live the entire year. Are we living those minutes by design or default?

Who would have thought that winning the lottery could hijack your life in anything other than a positive way? As I mentioned, Donna's story could just as well have been about losing a job or the home of your dreams. Winning the lottery bolted her out of the life she was building and put her into a life she felt she had no control over. Isn't that exactly what happens when we lose a job or we lose our home?

However, what a great opportunity in that Crystalline Moment to redefine who we are! Think about this...Donna would never have started the life she loves if her family had not won the lottery which had nothing to do with the $34.5 million. It had everything to do with her recognizing the opportunity that she was being given and taking the baby steps to design the life she loves.

If you are facing an unknown future after the loss of a job, take the time to write down everything you would love to do, then read them out loud to yourself or someone else. Which of those things give *you* life? Which of the possibilities make you feel lighter, more expanded? When I am talking with coaching clients or just people in random and I ask them what they would love to do, I can tell instantly by the inflection of their voice if it truly is what they would love...what they are passionate about! When we write down our dreams and then say them out loud, we activate our entire brain and the answers will start to become clear.

Does that mean everything will happen instantly? Of course not! Just because we have a Crystalline Moment and see the opportunity doesn't mean there isn't work to be done. The first important part of living the life of our dreams is to recognize and define what that is. It may take years for us to bridge the gap of our dream life from where we are starting, but we will never get there if we can't define what that is and then design the bridge to cross the gap.

What a story Karen has from childhood abuse to successful educator and entrepreneur! Her commitment, she says, is what got her from victim to achiever. There are several stories of abuse in this book. The one thing that all of the people have in common is their commitment to achieving the life of their dreams.

They all talk about "baby" Crystalline Moments. Karen, Andrew, Ann and the amazing ladies from South Africa all recognize the journey. If you are experiencing some type of abuse or someone in your family is, one of the things that can get you through it is taking those baby steps.

Find support and ask for the help you need. Find a source that provides hope and inspiration to you. It could be something you read or watch on TV. It could also be an organization or individual you follow online. You will recognize your own Crystalline Moments when you take those baby steps, whether it is getting out of an abusive relationship or dealing with addiction. For Andrew, it was an eagle that changed the direction of his life. What is your eagle?

Another important aspect in almost all of these stories is learning to listen to that inner voice. Kathie talks about the voice as the Creator of the Universe speaking to her. Others will say it is God speaking to them, intuition or the Universe. No matter what you want to call it, if you give space to that inner voice, it has a great power to guide you. The Crystalline Moment moves us into taking action and stepping into the opportunities that are laid out before us. We have a choice - we can say yes or no to that opportunity. If Denise had not listened to her inner voice, she would not be alive.

As I stated before, I used to fight with my inner voice and it never paid off. My ego or thinking would override what that inner voice would tell me. The problem is never the *problem*, it is always the *thinking* about the problem. That was my problem - my thinking or rationale would override what the Universe was trying to tell me. If we pause and get quiet so we can hear what that little voice is telling us, it will guide us into the direction of the life we are meant to have.

The more we listen to that inner voice, the easier it becomes. Remember what Oprah says, first a pebble, then a stone, then a boulder, then a brick wall. It is much better to listen to that pebble than wait for the brick wall that is guaranteed to show up.

Rob has a very high capacity to listen to that inner voice that has guided him to have a company that can serve people that need help with a down payment for their homes. What a wonderful thing that has resulted in his ability to listen to his inner voice and help thousands with the home of their dreams! He is creating Crystalline Moments for many because he listened to his own moments. The same is true for everyone in this book.

Kathie and Julie Renee have amazing stories of overcoming huge physical obstacles. Both were told they would never walk again and are living amazing lives today. They are great stories of how what appears to be impossible is possible. We need to find the frequency of the life we are supposed to live, then we can achieve the impossible or as Taylor says, become extraordinary.

If we are watching CBS on TV and we want to watch the Discovery Channel, we just change the channel. The same is true in living the lives of our dreams. If we adjust the frequency of our thoughts to be at the energy level of our dreams, then things will start to happen that take us across the gap. Those are our Crystalline Moment opportunities.

We talked about Ralph Waldo Emerson's quote called *The Experiment*:

"I have learned....that if one advances confidently in the direction of their dream, endeavoring to live the life they are imagining, one passes an invisible boundary..."

An important word in this quote is *'endeavoring'*, that means it will not be a perfect life where we don't have fear, failure and challenges. When these things happen, stop and address what is really going on. Notice what you are noticing, then make any adjustments necessary.

Karel talks about someone showing up in her life just when she was going through regrets and failures in the relationships she had with her husband and family. Many others I have had conversations with in addition to people in this book talk about someone showing up at that very moment and defining the direction they were meant to go.

Emerson goes on to say, *"...all sorts of things begin to occur that never otherwise would have occurred."*

No matter what your dream, once you are wearing your dream, things will happen that help you bridge your gap. The important thing is to believe and live your life as if your dream has already happened. The Crystalline Moments will be there to help you move into your dream. Little things will happen out of nowhere.

When I decided I wanted to first become a DreamBuilder coach then later a Life Mastery Consultant, it was a major financial investment. I had no idea where that money was going to come from. What I did know was this was the life I wanted to live. What was amazing is that where I thought the money was going to come from never happened. But because I was stepping into my dream and following the direction the Crystalline Moments were taking me, the money appeared in unexpected forms that just appeared. Did I have to sacrifice a little? Yes. Did I have to adjust to new ways of doing things? Absolutely! We have to let go of our old ways as change doesn't happen without adjustments.

I would like to say one thing about our money paradigms. I was raised in a family that lived in lack. My parents were incredible parents and I owe my tenacity to my mother, but I was raised on a farm where we had no money. My paradigm when it comes to money was always that of constriction so even when I was doing well, there was always something waiting for me to block me moving beyond that paradigm. The wonderful thing that has happened is that now that I am living my life's purpose and dreams, I now recognize the money paradigm and continue to change that pattern. I'm not perfect at it but the most important thing is to recognize when it is happening and change the thought pattern.

If you have a money paradigm that stops you from moving forward in the life you know you are meant to live, recognize that it is just that - a paradigm and a pattern that can be changed.

Now I feel nothing but joy when I am helping others discover the life of their dreams and then watching them blossom and put that dream in motion. What is interesting is that in my past, the Universe had been trying to tell me this and I wasn't listening.

I have loved training hundreds of sales people and showing entrepreneurs how to have successful businesses. Now when I look back, that was the Universe preparing me for this wonderful incredible life that is now unfolding for me, just as Ginny talks about losing loved ones in her life was preparing her for the loss of her two children. If my husband had not passed, I would never have looked for a "new life". I would never have changed my life philosophy. I would never have written this book that I am so passionate about.

Let's look at the inspirational stories of Kevin, Kenzie and Taylor. All three of these individuals seem to seamlessly listen and follow the Crystalline Moments of their lives. They listen to that inner voice and are living the lives of their dreams and exactly what Emerson says in the rest of his quote,

"...One begins to meet with a success unexpected in common hours. New more Universal, more liberal Laws begin to establish themselves around this person or the old Laws are rearranged in one's favor, nevertheless, one begins to live with a license of a higher order of being."

Does that mean that Kevin, Kenzie and Taylor are not going to have challenges? Emphatically, NO! As Kevin talks about finding the route up the Dawn Wall, he and his teammate had to make adjustments. We all have to make adjustments as we take the steps toward our dreams. That is what those little Crystalline Moments are all about. We need to pause and see what the next step is. Sometimes it may mean that our dream needs an adjustment or we are not quite in alignment with our life's purpose.

Tricia continues to call and tell me about the amazing Crystalline Moments that are happening. Just imagine having your own paintings in a gallery where the painting appeared exactly as it was described in the book you're writing, sight unseen! There are no accidents in our lives...just Crystalline Moments and their opportunities.

What is the Universe saying to you? Do you identify with any of the stories in this book? You too can examine the Crystalline Moments in your life and put your dream life on. There are four phases to creating your dream life. All along the way, there will be Crystalline Moments to help direct you up your own Dawn Wall.

Phase 1 - Create the seed of your Dream by first discovering your dream. Next is designing and testing your dream, then recognizing that you deserve your dream.

Phase 2 - Create a bridge over the gap between the life you know and the life you love. In order to create that bridge, you must learn how to befriend your fear, create abundance with gratitude and giving where there is lack and then evolve your perceptions. You will need to learn how to re-pattern your life.

Phase 3 - Putting on your Dream by listening to that small inner voice where the Crystalline Moments are, then harness the power of believing. This means that if you can't believe in the dream, you need to have someone that can believe for you until *you* believe it is possible. Then turn any failures into stepping stones.

Phase 4 - Celebrate the harvesting of your Dream. The real gift is way more than the Dream you have created. It is really about the gift of who YOU became in the process. Your Dream life is fluid. I equate it to a business plan or goal setting. Your Dream life will create new Crystalline Moments that creates new opportunities so that you continue to grow and expand.

From these phases, here are 5 steps you can take right now to find your opportunities.

1. First, take some time to think about what Crystalline Moments you have had in your past or that you may be having right now. Define those moments in as much detail as possible by writing them down.

2. Choose one of the moments and read what you have written out loud to yourself. What are the emotions or feelings you are having as you read it? Define those feelings and emotions by writing them down.

3. Now read what you have written about your feelings. Tune into what your inner voice is saying as you read them. Do not use your thinking; use your gut. What gives you life, or what stands out?

4. What are some possible opportunities that could be waiting for you from those moments? When you write those down and read them out loud, which one makes you feel expansive and more alive?

5. What is an affirmation you can use to step into that opportunity? Write that down and put it somewhere that you will see frequently.

To make this process easy for you, I have created a "Crystalline Moments Toolkit" you can download for free. It will help you discover your moments and what opportunities they present in your life.

Simply go to www.CrystallineMoments.com, then register using this code: MyMoments. You will then have access to your Crystalline Moment Toolkit. You will also be able to see other stories that I will be sharing. If you would like to share your story, you can contact me on the website. You can also join our conversation by going to the Crystalline Moments Facebook page as well. I look forward to seeing you there.

I cannot describe to you the passion and joy from which this book has been written. I am filled with love and gratitude for these and all of the other amazing people that are contributing to my quest to help you discover what your Crystalline Moments can do for your life.

I hope you too can, *"Have Fun, Give Back, Make Money!"*

About the Author

For over 30 years, Coni has worked with organizations and individuals. She helped build two companies from small startups to a national presence. She has owned four companies of her own.

Coni has helped individuals and organizations in sales and marketing around the country reach their dreams in the housing and insurance industries. She has shown her clients how they then can do the same for their customers and clients, and has worked closely with top coaches and trainers in the industry to promote their programs and courses.

She received the prestigious Life Mastery Consultant certification through the Life Mastery Institute. This advanced certification, along with her experience and knowledge, helps to propel others to new heights creating richer, more fulfilling lives and...**turning their dreams into destiny!**

Made in the USA
San Bernardino, CA
16 April 2017